Joe cautiously approached the low bed and kneeled down beside it, trying to reason out the situation. Remy's arms were wedged close to her body. He expertly felt her wrist. When he tried to lay her arm in a better position to check again, he could not move it. He let go instantly and nervously brought his fingers through his thick black hair, pushing it back from his worried brow.

Joe went on to ask the often asked question of a fainting victim: "How do you feel?" But, for some unexplainable reason, the question came out, "Who are you?"

Remy's body stirred slightly and her mouth began to move.

"I am Teresita Basa!" The Voice was strong and vibrant. Chills went up and down Joe's spine. It was not Remy's voice, of that Joe was certain . . .

———

Written with the full cooperation of Remy and Joe Chua, the people who lived these events, this compelling book reveals the bizarre occurrences of possession that led to the arrest of a murderer— and the ordeal of the woman chosen to speak for a murder victim . . .

———

A VOICE FROM THE GRAVE

A VOICE FROM THE GRAVE

Carol Mercado

BERKLEY BOOKS, NEW YORK

A VOICE FROM THE GRAVE

A Berkley Book / published by arrangement with the authors

PRINTING HISTORY
Carolando Press edition published 1979
Diamond edition / June 1994
Berkley edition / March 1996

The Putnam Berkley World Wide Web site address is
http://www.berkley.com

ISBN: 0-425-15511-0

BERKLEY®
Berkley Books are published by The Berkley Publishing Group,
200 Madison Avenue, New York, New York 10016.
BERKLEY and the "B" design
are trademarks belonging to Berkley Publishing Corporation.

PRINTED IN THE UNITED STATES OF AMERICA

10 9 8 7 6 5 4 3 2 1

*This one is for
Teresita*

Acknowledgments

This story could not have been told without the cooperation of Joe and Remy Chua; investigators Joseph Stachula and Lee Epplen; Lt. Warren Whalen; Ron Somera and so many other people who helped but wished to remain anonymous. Finally, a special thanks to our editor, L. M. Johnston.

The story of **A Voice From the Grave** is *true*! The names and descriptions of the main characters in the story are their own. Some other names as well as identifying descriptions were changed; sometimes a composite of two or more individuals was used to protect their privacy. To allow for better story flow the sequence in which some of the events took place was slightly changed.

1

Teresita Basa pulled back the drapes slightly and looked out the front window of her fifteenth floor apartment high above the narrow congested street on Chicago's North Shore. Evening falls early during the month of February, so she was too late to catch the setting sun. The light from the room cast back on the window and mirrored an image. Teresita's dark auburn hair and Spanish eyes were complemented by the bright red sweater she was wearing. Although the many days of snow flurries had subsided and today's weather had been deceptively sunny, there had been no real change in the repetitively frigid weather since November.

Teresita had been here for many years, but she still found it difficult coping with the cold, unrelenting winters. The harsh weather, combined with annoyances at work that day, put her in a dismal mood. She shivered. Bringing her crossed arms up, she rubbed each hand vigorously on her upper arms trying to ward off the chill of the view. "Dios Mio," she thought, "I've got to pull myself out of this mood." She abruptly shut the drapes shielding herself from the oppressive winter gray skies.

Turning back towards her living room, she walked in the direction of her stereo cabinet that was built into the booklined wall adjacent to the dining area. She brushed past the television set that was in the way. The back cover was on the floor tilted against the set. She hoped it could be fixed tonight because the Boston Philharmonic was going to be on Channel 11. Mondays were so boring, otherwise.

Reaching the cabinet, she pulled open the louvered doors and proceeded to flip through her well stocked record collection. She knew that music would soothe her frustration. Music was the pinnacle of her life. She had been studying music since she was a child in the Philippines and later continued her studies in Europe and the United States. In spite of her extensive classical training, she enjoyed all types of music. She selected an album by Mantovani.

When the music began permeating the room, she walked over to the couch, eased her slight frame down, and plumped a pillow behind her back. She flipped off her slippers and drew up her feet on the cushions. Leaning her head back and closing her eyes, she began absorbing the soothing vibrations of the Mantovani music.

As she began to relax, a kaleidoscope of tranquil scenes began to reflect in her mind. She visualized her mother silhouetted against the background of her home on Negros Island. She saw the crystal blue skies of the Pacific and the sandy palm-lined beaches with alternating slap-stroke, slap-stroke of the ocean waves. As her thoughts continued to flow forth, she envisioned the music book she was planning to write.

The telephone rang, jarring her back to the present.

"Oh, hi, Sarah! What am I doing? Nothing right at the moment but I'm expecting someone later."

"Anyone I know?" inquired Sarah.

"Maybe," she answered, being purposely evasive.

"In that case, I'll let you go Teresita."

"No! No! I have time. I was just relaxing right now." She continued, "I had another frustrating day at the hospital. I don't know why the supervisor gives me all the emergency cases to do in the respiratory department."

"Teresita, you should really consider going back to teaching."

"You know how it is Sarah, I've been away from teaching for awhile and getting a job at a university in the music department is just too difficult without tenure."

"Well, maybe after you finish your book, you'll get job offers. How is it coming, by the way?"

"It's coming along. . . ." The doorbell rang. "Excuse me, Sarah, someone's at the door, you want to hang on while I answer?"

"No, we'll talk later, Teresita, bye now."

Putting the receiver down, Teresita hurried to the door and looked out the tiny peephole giving a distorted panoramic view of the outside hallway. She recognized the face outside the door at once. She removed the safety chain and unlocked the door, allowing the caller into her apartment.

Turning her back on the visitor, she closed the door and slipped the safety chain back. Out of the corner of her eye she caught the quick blurring movement of an arm grabbing her from behind. Before Teresita could react the strong arm encircled her neck in a Japanese half-nelson. As the arm jerked back, her body raised up and then thrust forward, accentuating the effect of the choke hold, and instantly her body fell limply into unconsciousness.

2

Satisfied that Teresita was unconscious, the intruder let her body drop to the floor.

Wasting no time, he reached for her purse which was sitting on the coffee table. Looking inside, he found thirty dollars. He quickly took the money and pushed it into his pants pocket and slung the purse near the couch.

Walking back to the unconscious Teresita, he placed his strong fingers under her armpits and dragged the body to the bedroom, hurling it on the floor next to the bed. He peeled away the sweater and slacks and stripped off her underclothes, and then positioned the naked body on its back.

Moving quickly now, he went to the kitchen. Pulling open some drawers, he spotted the knives. He drew out a large wooden-handled butcher knife.

He walked back to the bedroom. Placing one foot on either side of her hips, he straddled the body. Dropping to his knees, he bent over the woman. Pressing his index finger to the body, he outlined the sternum and carefully brought the point of the knife to the soft yielding space between the ribs and rested it against the target. He hesitated for a moment. One hand was tightly gripping the wooden handle while the other hand stood ready a fraction of an inch above the heel of the knife handle. Then, mustering all of his strength, he lunged forward plunging the knife deep into Teresita.

The knife was driven with such force that its handle was embedded in the flesh, depressing the chest wall and forcing air out of the woman's lungs which caused a loud gasp to escape from her lips. The gasp startled the perspiring killer. Springing up from the floor and backing away quickly from the body, he avoided getting the pulsating blood on his hands and clothes.

Without looking back at the woman, he went to the dresser and rummaged through one drawer after another but found nothing of value. Flipping open the jewelry box, he poured the contents on top of the dresser. He looked at the jewelry for a moment, eyeing a ring and pendant and then scooped all of it into his coat pocket. He went on ransacking the rest of the apartment but could not find anything else he could plunder.

Returning to the bedroom, he stared down at the cold, lifeless body. The bleeding had stopped and the blood was beginning to coagulate. He reached down and forced her legs open.

Looking around the room, he spied a paper bag. He picked it up and crushed it in his hand. He reached into his pocket, pulled out his lighter and lit the bag. He then threw the blazing mass on top of the mattress. He waited for the mattress to catch on fire, and with one quick jerk propelled the mattress on top of the body.

Making a hasty retreat out of the room, the killer headed for the front door. Pausing for a moment to catch his breath, he unhooked the safety chain, unlocked the door and quietly walked out of the apartment.

"Thirty lousy bucks, that fuckin' bitch!" thought the embittered killer as he fingered the wadded bills that he had hurriedly stuffed into his pants pocket. He had been lucky. No one had seen him come or go. As he proceeded south on Pine Grove Avenue, he was cautious to walk at an inconspicuous pace. When he rounded the corner, his pace quickened. He zipped his jacket and pulled up the collar to protect his neck and face from the biting cold wind blustering off Lake Michigan.

He was now two blocks away from the murder scene and he felt safe. Focusing on his thoughts, he continued his pace. "Here I am running around doing these errands for her like some nigger and this is what I get." He headed west towards Clark Street. In the distance, he could see the glaring headlights of the commuting cars. He passed a storefront bar and was tempted to stop for a beer but thought better of it and continued on his way.

Soon his mind was reeling again. "I'm going here and there with her—helping her get her citizenship papers. Hell, I thought she had money the way everyone around the hospital talked about how rich her family was—and that television set, I could have fixed it! All I had to do was check out which modular board she needed. Those repairmen don't know what they're doing."

He jammed his cold hands in his jacket pockets and angrily clinched the jewelry in his fist. "You'd think she'd at least have some diamonds," he thought indignantly. "I'll have to go through this jewelry tomorrow and see if there's anything to sell. That ring and pendant aren't bad, but the rest is junk. I'll have to dump it."

He was almost to Clark Street when he heard the high-whining shrill sound of the fire truck's siren. He stopped for a moment, cocking his head towards the sound. A sadistic smile appeared on his dark angular face, and his lips silently formed the words, "You are too late you bastards!—too late!"

3

Hook and Ladder Engine 44 of the Chicago Fire Department swiftly made its way north on Clark Street, passing the row of cars that had quickly pulled to the side obediently responding to the urgent message of the siren. As they approached the intersection, the driver had to abruptly swerve to one side out of the way of a black sedan making a left turn. "Jesus, look at that," shouted the exasperated driver. He expertly turned the large steering wheel and maneuvered the truck back on its course. Turning to his companion, he angrily remarked, "What's the matter with these jerks, Lieutenant? Don't they know that they have to stop for a fire truck?"

Lieutenant Warren Whalen gave the driver a knowing nod, but his thoughts were concentrated on the fire scene. He knew the building was a high-rise and that the apartment was on the fifteenth floor. It might be too far up for their heavy equipment. He hoped it was a contained fire, otherwise, it could be trouble.

The vehicle made a quick right turn off Clark

Street into a small side street narrowly avoiding a collision with a double parked car on the corner. The driver swore under his breath as he downshifted. The icy streets made the driving more risky. The truck sped east on the darkened street for a few more blocks when Lt. Whalen motioned to the driver and said, "Slow it down, that's our street coming up." The driver turned south on the one-way street. Halfway down the block, Lt. Whalen noticed a large group of people milling in front of the 2740 high-rise. Judging from the way they were dressed, they were apparently tenants who had made a hasty exit from the building.

The lieutenant was off the truck before it came to a halt. Two firefighters quickly jumped off the back of the truck. Carrying five gallon hand pumps and hatchets, they joined the lieutenant. Together they moved towards the entrance of the building as the shivering crowd excitedly moved out of the way.

They were met in the lobby by the janitor, Peter Lulusa. It was Lulusa who had called the fire department after he had been notified by one of the tenants who had seen smoke seeping from under the door of Apartment 15B at about 8:30 p.m.

The janitor took the lieutenant and his men up in the elevator. When the doors opened, the small group moved down the hall towards Apartment 15B. Noticing the black smoke filtering underneath the front door, the lieutenant jerked off his glove and pressed his bare hand to the door. The surface was warm, not hot, so it seemed to indicate a smoldering localized fire. He instructed the janitor to open the door with the passkey. It was rare not to have a forced entry.

Lulusa nervously fumbled through a large key chain, and finding the right key, he carefully unlocked the door. When he opened the door, they were greeted by a billowing black cloud of smoke that poured from the apartment.

With a rehearsed move, the firefighters dropped to their knees and crawled on the floor avoiding the suffocating smoke hovering above. They made their way to the source of the fire which appeared to be in the bedroom. The other men were busy hooking up the hoses below. However, they were able to quickly extinguish the blaze with their hand pumps. The windows were opened throughout the apartment allowing the crisp cold air in to ventilate the room.

While smoke lifted, the firefighters began to overhaul the room, taking out the soggy clothes and blankets. As Lt. Whalen tugged on the mattress that had been burning, he felt a resistance. He tried but could not quite lift it. He turned to call for help, but one of the other men had seen him struggling and came to his assistance. With their combined strength, the two men were able to lift the water-soaked mattress from the floor.

It was then that the sickening stench rose above the acrid smell of the smoke to sting their nostrils—the unmistakable stench of burning flesh. There lying at their feet, wedged between the bottom of the bed and the wall, was the naked, charred remains of a human being. With a more careful look, they both noticed the handle of a knife jutting from the chest. Looking down at the pitiful sight the lieutenant whispered, "My God, what a horrible way to die." Then, turning to his partner, he said grimly, "Let's leave everything the way it is. This is a police matter!"

4

Police Officers Andruzzi, Russelle, and Sergeant Loftus were the first on the murder scene; however, the responsibility for the investigation of Teresita Basa's murder fell under the jurisdiction of Area 6 Homicide. Early Tuesday morning, Investigators O'Connor and Philbin were at the Basa apartment and prepared a preliminary report of the murder which headquarters would follow up with a full-fledged investigation.

Area 6 Homicide Section of the Chicago Police Department is headquartered in a modern two story L-shaped brick building. Outside, elongated stone steps lead from the city sidewalk to an expansive concrete courtyard. Towering in the center of the yard are three flagpoles flying the colors of the United States, the State of Illinois, and the City of Chicago. The ominous eyes of the cameras slowly pan back and forth, monitoring the activities surrounding the grounds and corridors of the building. These electronic sentinels placed in strategic locations around and inside the building are not hidden from view. The effect gives visitors the insidious warning that they are being carefully watched.

Beyond the glass faced entrance in the lobby, police in uniforms and plain clothes are passing by the information island. In the center of the island, a uniformed policewoman tends the telephones and closed-circuit screens. Behind the information area, the planked, angled stairway leads to the second floor. On the second floor, two large swinging doors with boldly printed letters reading "HOMICIDE AREA 6" open into an auditorium-sized room which occupies the west wing of the building. Immediately to the left of the entry, a policeman stands behind a long rectangular counter manning the data machines, telephones and a myriad of files. Encircling the room are a number of doors leading to small interrogation rooms and offices. The large room is filled with row after row of official looking gray metal tables and desks, each with a typewriter and coaster chair and a side chair for the interviewee.

This Tuesday night a number of detectives are scattered throughout the room, each busy with his own activity. Most are dressed in unobtrusive civilian clothes; some are in Levi's and sports shirts, and a couple are wearing disco type outfits. As one of the detectives is picking clothes out of a gunnysack, he shakes each piece and carefully examines it. Farther back, the overhead light beams down off the bald head of a detective with a scowl on his face finishing up a report. At another desk, an exasperated investigator is trying to type a report from the information that a young Hispanic male is giving, in between the sobbing interruptions of the youth's mother.

In the last row, at the right hand corner desk, sits a medium-sized, muscularly trim man with neatly combed salt and pepper hair. His chair is tilted back and one foot is wedged on the pedestal as his other foot dangles in the air. He is oblivious to the activity going on around the room as he reads from a manila file folder.

Homicide/Murder—Victim: Basa, Teresita 4–059 292 is printed on the front of the folder. The man reading the file is Investigator Joseph Stachula. He is looking at the preliminary report written by Detectives O'Connor and Philbin who had started the investigation earlier that day during their tour of duty. The case was now officially assigned to Stachula and his partner, Investigator Lee Epplen. Their job was to try to put the pieces of the puzzle together and find the perpetrator of the crime.

Epplen was questioning some of the victim's coworkers at Edgewater Hospital, and hopefully, he would get a good lead.

Stachula rubbed his chin with his hand as he studied the reports. From the looks of things, the case was a routine murder-rape crime. However, the way the body had been burned, it might be difficult for them to get much evidence.

He looked over the typed list of names and telephone numbers attached to the report. They were relatives and friends of the victim. Deciding on a course of action, he brought his feet down to the floor and pulled his chair closer to the desk. He picked up the phone and began dialing the first number on the list.

5

To Ron Somera, the cousin of Teresita, fell the difficult job of arranging for her remains to be shipped back to the Philippines. Teresita had meant a great deal to Somera, since she was the only close relative he had in Chicago. He found her to be a charming, sincere, and generous person, and he valued the times he and his family had spent with her.

It had just been on the Sunday before her death that she had played the piano with his combo at a hall. She had particularly enjoyed singing a duet of the hit song "Feelings" with Ron. They laughed and embraced as they breathlessly finished the last stanza of the song. Teresita had been happy then. It had been a wonderful moment he would treasure. He would always try to remember her in that glowing moment and not as a mass of burned human flesh cloaked in a white sheet, the way that he saw her Tuesday morning when he identified her corpse in the morgue.

Somera made the solemn arrangements: calling the undertakers, selecting the appropriate casket, filling out forms for the consulate and state department, and arranging the trip and transfers with the airlines.

By Thursday evening, Teresita took her last ride home.

The casket reached Manila on Friday morning, the 25th of February, 1977. By late afternoon, Teresita's remains arrived at her final destination, the city of Dumaguete.

Situated on the southern tip of Oriental Negros, an island in the Visayan region of the Philippines, Dumaguete is rich in Spanish heritage and tradition, the results of four centuries of Spanish rule.

Although it is a city of over 30,000 people, Dumaguete embodies a small town atmosphere. It has not changed much since Teresita's childhood. The Catholic Church with its double dome and historical belfry stands dominantly in the center of town. In front of the church is a large recreational plaza with lush banana, mango, and beautiful acacia trees casting friendly shadows on long wooden benches. Here the town people can congregate in the early evening to exchange pleasantries, expound their political views, and trade the latest news and gossip.

As a teenager, Teresita and her girlfriends spent many wonderful times promenading around the terrazzo plaza under the watchful eyes of their chaperones. Those were the years shortly after the Second World War when all around the island there was an air of excitement and national purpose as talk of Philippine independence intensified.

This evening, there had been a folk dance in the plaza. With the young men in the group attired in their traditional Baron Tagalog, the stiffly starched white linen shirt worn outside the slacks, and the beautiful young ladies resplendent in their colorful dresses with the fitted bodice, puffed sleeves, and flowing gathered skirts, the Patajong was performed on the crowded plaza. One of the folk dances that the audience enthusiastically responded to was the Tinikling. The dancers adeptly jumped in and out between two long bamboo poles, rhythmically slapped together to the beat of the music.

The crowd dispersed after the show. While the older people took a refreshing stroll on the boulevard lined with acacia trees by the sea, the young people, the ones in the traditional costumes, some conventionally dressed, and others wearing Levi's and tee-shirts imprinted with the latest slang, mingled and talked on the plaza.

The plaza provides a romantic backdrop for the town's youth where many exchange romantic words and secret promises, yet tonight the talk was not so much of romance, but of the harsh realities of life. One of their members had been murdered in the United States. Teresita's death helped to solidify in their minds Chicago's malevolent reputation.

Under one of the plaza's bright lamps, a small group of young people from nearby Silliman University gathered around a well worn wooden bench. One of the students, Raul, was sitting on the back-rest of the bench while he rested his Adidas-encased feet on the seat.

He talked and gestured saying, "The Basa family have always been important in Dumaguete. You see that monument over there," pointing to the marble obelisk standing at one end of the plaza. "The name of her godfather is carved there. He was one of the liberators of the Philippines during the Spanish-American War and her uncle was in the first Philippine Congress shortly after we gained our independence from the States."

Raul went on, "She was a classical pianist, and she taught music at our University." He was articulating what he had heard all that week from his mother who had known Teresita well and his father, a town official. "She studied at the Royal Conservatory of Music in London. In fact, in England she lived in the home of the Philippine ambassador at the court of St. James while she attended school there."

"But what was she doing in Chicago?" asked Rosita, sitting to the right of Raul on the bench. She was wearing her long hair swept back and held in place with an intricately carved tortoiseshell comb. The streetlight illuminated her high cheekbones and accented her natural beauty, so it took Raul a few seconds longer than usual to reply, "Well, you know that her father, Judge Basa, died a few years ago. He died from some sort of respiratory disease. Teresita was very upset about it and decided she would try to help other people with breathing problems, so she went to school and became an inhalation therapist. She was working in a large Chicago hospital at the time she was killed."

Roberto, another member of the group who had been standing to the left of Raul, asked, "She never married, did she?"

"No," answered Raul, "I guess she never found the right man."

"Oh no," countered Rosita, she was standing up now looking at Raul, "I bet she found the right man once. But you know how these strict old Spanish families are. They probably disapproved of him. Poor lady, what a sad way to end a life."

A short distance away from the plaza is the Basas' main house, a large imposing white structure built in the traditional Spanish architecture common to the region. The house is set behind in portillo, an archway with heavy wrought iron gates guarding the entrance to the patio. All around the house there is an abundance of tropical trees, foliage, and great varieties of flowers that bloom profusely all year round.

The house stood for more than shelter and comfort from the elements. While most houses were ordinarily constructed from wood with roofs made of galvanized metal or nipa, palm leaves, the Basas' great homes were indicative of wealth and position since the family had considerable holdings in sugar and coconut plantations.

As an only child of one of the island's elite families, Teresita was brought up in a sheltered household. She was looked after by many muchachas who cooked, cleaned, and washed and ironed for the family.

Her early school years were spent at St. Paul's College, a Catholic high school in Dumaguete. When the time came for college, Teresita was sent to Manila to study music at St. Scholastica an exclusive girls college run by an order of German nuns.

There was nothing at all in Teresita's gentle affluent background that would prepare her for the brutal end that she met.

In the gloom that had befallen the Basa household, the help was working busily in the kitchen preparing the food that would be needed for the three days of Pabasa, the prayers following the funeral. They were talking among themselves and expressing a great deal of concern for the Señora, Teresita's mother.

The Señora was in her bedroom upstairs trying to rest in her large mahogany bed. The sedation that the doctor had given her earlier had done nothing to bring her the much needed sleep. Her head lay on the pillow, and her eyes gazed up at the ceiling as she recalled the warnings that she had given Teresita. She had been opposed to Teresita's desire to stay in Chicago.

She could not understand why Teresita had wanted to leave Dumaguete. Teresita had everything here that she could want, her friends, relatives, and there were servants of the household at her command. Teresita should have stayed. She belonged here, by her mother.

The Señora's face was saturated with perspiration and she could feel the heavy erratic beat of her heart. She prayed that she could find the strength to carry on for the next few days. Her heart was badly damaged by the trauma brought on from the news of Teresita's death and particularly the manner in which she died.

PHILIPPINES

Philippine Sea

Tuguegarao

LUZON

South China Sea

Quezon
City

Manila

MINDORO

SAMAR

PANAY

CEBU LEYTE

NEGROS BOHOL

Dumaguete

MINDANAO

SCALE

100   200   300 Miles

0   100   200   300   400 Kilometers

6

On Saturday morning the church was crowded with family, friends, and townspeople who had come to pray at the funeral mass. The simple sealed casket lay at the foot of the altar while the priest gave his blessings.

Inside the church, the litany of prayers and sorrowful cries intermingled in the air, reverberating from the cavernous ceiling creating a low murmur-like echo throughout the church.

After the mass, the mourners slowly filed by the casket of Teresita to pay their last respects. Crossing themselves as they passed, several stopped to lay freshly cut flowers on the casket, and many women tearfully clutching their rosary beads stood before the casket for a few moments as their lips moved in silent prayer.

Señora Basa, wearing the black mourning dress and veil that had been her uniform since the passing of her husband, sat silently in her pew at the front of the church. Tears of pain and rage swelled up in her eyes while she watched the procession of people passing by her daughter's casket. Her heart felt heavy with the thought that she would never again see her daughter. She longed for one last look at Teresita since it was tradition on the Islands to have a closed casket with a small glass window by the face of the deceased to allow their loved ones a last look, but there was no glass window on Teresita's casket. There could not be one. The beast who had taken her life had seen to it that she was burned beyond recognition.

It was noon by the time the funeral procession got under way. Leading the procession was a funeral band with metered drum beats and wailing trumpets. Behind them were the priest and two altar boys carefully holding up the church's golden crucifix. Next came Señora Basa, who in spite of her family's and doctor's warnings walked with family members in front of the casket. It was carried by relatives and close friends of Teresita. Following the casket, walking four abreast, came the long lines of friends and townspeople.

Slowly, the mournful procession made its way around the plaza, then turned right at the corner into Alfonso Trece Street, past the municipio, the town hall, and continued up the winding streets towards the cemetery. A few blocks later they were at the outskirts of town. Columns of coconut palms lined the road to the cemetery. The procession entered the large gates of the cemetery and made their way towards the Basa family plot.

The grave diggers had done their work the night before and the freshly dug grave awaited Teresita's casket. The priest said a short prayer and gave his final blessing. As the casket was ceremoniously lowered into the ground there were outbursts of crying.

Señora Basa was taken by her family to a waiting car which sped away to her home for some much needed rest. The priest, other family members, and close friends would go directly to the Basa household for the Pabasa. The rest of the mourners would stop at least once during the three days of prayers to give their condolences to the Señora.

With the crowd slowly dispersing, the grave diggers began filling the grave. One man, a graying proud Filipino, stayed behind, lost in silent prayer. The diggers carefully prepared the top soil, rolled back the sod, and draped the wreaths beside the burial place. The flowers' scents pervaded the air. Finishing their work the diggers quickly departed, leaving the old man all alone by the grave.

The man was Adriano, the Basa family jardinero for over forty years. He had known Señorita Teresita since she was a small child. He vividly remembered how the beautiful sound of her piano would filter throughout the house and out to the gardens as he worked.

Adriano moved closer to the grave and bent down to place on the grass the delicate orchids that he had cut from the garden that morning. He had patiently taught Teresita the names of the tropical plants. The orchids were Teresita's favorite flowers, and he vowed that he would return often to bring these flowers to her grave.

Adriano's stubby fingers wiped away the tears that paused at the crevices of his weathered face.

"Dios Mio, Dios Mio," he prayed. "Please let

there be justice. Please help find the animal who did this vile deed."

It was then that he felt a cold chill on his back and arms. Underneath his work boots, he felt a deep stirring in the ground beneath. The old man had lived on the Island all of his life and he was not frightened by things he could not understand, but at that very moment he fell to his knees. With his eyes closed, he whispered a prayer, "Please dear god, Ayuda, Ayuda—help Teresita rest. Help her rest."

7

Investigator Joseph Stachula lifted out a stack of folders from under a tan brief case on his desk. As he sat shuffling through the folders, he decided to check the Basa case to see if any new data had been filed. He pulled out the folder and laid it open on top of the stack. Inside, he found a group of Xerox papers stapled together. On the top sheet was written: *Pathological and protocol—Cook County Medical Examiner—Basa, Teresita—Autopsy Report.*

He began flipping through the report under the capitalized headings that read: General Description; Gross Anatomical Findings; Cavity Contents. These headings were followed by long technical descriptions of the forensic pathologist's findings. He stopped at the heading: Primary Incision Correlation.

He clasped his hands behind his neck and leaned back as he continued to read the page. He was in deep concentration when Lee Epplen, a tall, well-built man, walked out from the interrogation room immediately to the left of Stachula. "Listen Joe," he said as he looked through the black spiral notebook containing information he had compiled. "I've just been on the phone for two hours, and everyone says the same thing about the Basa woman."

"What do they say?" he automatically replied with his thoughts still concentrated on the report.

"They all say that she was a super lady."

Epplen shoved over the stack of folders and papers on Stachula's desk and sat down on the corner.

"Why don't you sit down?" said Joe somewhat sarcastically.

"Thanks," replied Lee. Ignoring Joe's remark, he went on. "In fact, I was just talking with . . ."—he hesitated momentarily while he found the name in his notes—"Dr. Antonio Blanco. He couldn't say enough about how wonderful Teresita was and how she had loaned him money to get his practice started. Joe, as far as I have been able to find out, the woman didn't have an enemy in the world."

"No enemies you say?" Joe retorted, bolting back to a sitting position. He handed Lee the Xeroxed copies of the autopsy report. While Lee silently skimmed quickly over the report, Joe said cynically, "I wouldn't call skewing someone to the floor with a butcher knife an act of fellowship, would you?"

They had worked together for a long time, so Epplen instinctively knew Stachula would clarify his metaphor with a more concise statement, and he rapped back a redundant answer, "Well no, but most rape-murder cases have nothing to do with enemies, Joe."

Raising his voice in a slightly quizzical tone, Joe replied, "A rape-murder, is that what we have? Murder . . . obviously, but there is definitely one thing wrong with the rape theory." He reached over to the pages of the report and pointed to the line: *Female Genital Tract—Intact hymen*. His voice dropped, "At age 48, Teresita Basa was a virgin."

8

It was 2:00 a.m. on the graveyard shift, and Remy Chua had a break from her assignments in the respiratory therapy department. She did not have to administer a treatment for another hour, so she took the opportunity to catch up on some rest.

While she headed down the corridor towards the locker room where the staff customarily took their breaks, she thought to herself, "I don't know why I said that to Jennie." As she shook her head mentally scrutinizing the remark, a hairpin fell, and, catching it at the temple, she placed it back in her dark brown upswept hair.

She had just been down the hall near the elevator, talking to her co-workers. They had all been discussing Teresita Basa's murder. The news of Teresita's death had shocked the staff in the respiratory department of Edgewater Hospital.

While they were talking down the corridor, Jennie Prince, the technical director of the department had said, "Can you imagine that? It's been two weeks and the police don't have any clues to Teresita's murder. She must be turning in her grave. Too bad she can't tell the police who did it!" Everyone nodded their heads in agreement.

Remy had jokingly interjected, "Jennie, if there is no solution to her murder, she can come to me in a dream—or she can appear. I'm not afraid."

Everyone in the group had a good laugh about it and after a few more moments of idle talk, the group slowly dispersed, returning to their respective assignments.

Remy wondered why she had made that remark to Jennie because she had not meant to joke about the murder, but they had all been disturbed by the thought that someone they knew could have been killed so brutally. However, she was glad that her remark had eased some of the tension in the department.

Entering the locker room, Remy took special care to push the heavy door back against the doorstop. She went to the far wall opposite the lockers and pulled out one of the chairs from the neatly lined row. Turning the chair around and situating it a couple of feet in front of one of the other slantbacked chairs, Remy sat down and propped her tired feet on the other seat. She had an excellent vantage point from that position to keep an eye on the door in case anyone needed her. Besides, she felt more secure with the door wide open.

Lying back on the chair, she moved her petite body back and forth trying to find a comfortable position. Soon she began to rest and her head dropped to one shoulder and then rolled forward towards her chest as she began falling into a quasi-sleep.

Her eyelids were almost closed when she sensed her head bobbing slowly up and down and side to side. The slow recurrent movement appeared to be conducted by a message emanating from the recess of her subconscious mind, warning her of some unknown peril. Gradually, the message filtered through and Remy began to awaken from her somnolent state.

Through the vented opening of her eyelids, she observed a subtle figure emerging in front of her. Remy was startled. She blinked, thinking at first that one of the nurses had entered the room. She looked again, focusing her eyes more clearly on the form. What she saw made her instinctively bring her right hand up to her forehead, down to her chest, across to her heart and over to the right shoulder, repeatedly forming the sign of the cross.

There, looking straight at her, was TERESITA BASA!

It was not a transparent or superimposed image but what appeared to be a real person. Teresita was shrouded in white and her delicate face wore a serene expression. She was close enough and real enough to touch.

But Remy did not reach for Teresita. Instead, she shoved the chair out of the way with her feet and jumped out of her seat and ran down the corridor towards the therapy department's main room. There under the bright fluorescent lights, Rudy Velasco, a fellow Filipino, was sitting down, carefully adjusting the apparatus on his respiratory therapy machine.

"Rudy! Rudy!" the pale and shaking Remy cried out, "I just saw Teresita in the locker room."

Remembering Remy's remarks earlier in the evening, Rudy looked up from his work and immediately began to laugh. "Oh, Mrs. Chua, Teresita is gone. Her body was sent back to the Philippines. How can she come back?

"She is dead, Mrs. Chua, she is dead!"

9

A month had passed since Teresita's murder. Remy was working overtime at the hospital from 11:00 p.m. to 11:00 a.m. because she and her husband were in the process of buying another home. The situation at work had become strained especially since Remy felt the night supervisor had been giving her most of the difficult cases to handle. These patients required constant care. This gave her little time to rest during the shift. In a sense, she was not unhappy about the added work because it acted as a diversion from her frequent thoughts about Teresita. She had been really shaken by the apparition.

Earlier that evening, she had been complaining to one of her fellow therapists, Florencio Oliver, about the heavy work load she had been assigned. Florencio stopped her in the middle of her sentence and said, "Mrs. Chua, the way you are talking and nagging—why, you are like the dead lady."

Remy feigned being mad and sharply replied, "Don't compare me to her, Florencio!" She grabbed a small wastepaper basket and jokingly threw it in his direction. Florencio caught the basket in mid-air and chuckled good naturedly. As he left the room, Remy had the strange feeling that maybe he was not kidding.

A couple of days later, her anxiety was augmented by an incident that occurred while talking to Emil Salvane, the night supervisor.

As Remy checked over her machine getting it prepared for the next patient, Emil hesitantly confided, "Did you hear, Mrs. Chua, that I had been questioned by the police in the murder case? But," he added quickly, "I don't think they think I'm involved."

Remy was shocked. She had known Emil since she had started working at Edgewater Hospital. Emil was a native of Haiti and he spoke English with the curious accentuated manner common to his island. He was well liked and respected. Remy had found Emil to be a perfect gentleman.

While they continued to talk, Remy wheeled her IPPB machine down the corridor. They stopped when they reached the elevator door. Remy pressed the up button and impatiently tapped her fingers against the metal plate and watched the light indicators blinking from floor to floor. Finally, the elevator arrived and she entered with the machine. She turned around and faced Emil and said emphatically, "Emil, you didn't do it. I know you didn't do it."

As the elevator doors were closing, Emil abruptly shoved his hand in between the doors forcing them to halt and then open. There was a frightened look in Emil's eyes as they riveted on hers. "Mrs. Chua, the way you just looked at me . . . the way you are

acting . . . my god, you seem just like Teresita."
Emil slowly removed his hand allowing the doors to
close.

The elevator reached Remy's floor. The doors
opened and she carefully maneuvered her machine
out into the corridor and down towards the patient's
room. As she passed the nurses' station, she noticed
that the front desk was unattended. She thought to
herself that the nurses were probably in the rooms
caring for patients or in the back room drinking
coffee and catching up with the charts.

She carefully opened the door and looked into the
room and quietly rolled in the machine. In the room,
reflected under the dim night light was the shape of
a man with his back propped up to a sitting position
on the bed. His mouth was open and he wheezed and
gasped frantically for air. His eyes opened and closed
as his barrel chest moved up and down with each
laborious breath.

Remy moved the Intermittent Positive Pressure
Breathing machine next to the bed and plugged it
into the oxygen outlet. This was going to be the
fourth treatment today for the patient, so she did not
have to go into a long explanation about procedure.
The man had emphysema. He could take a deep
breath but could not exhale all the accumulated
carbon dioxide. Taking the mask from its holder, she
held it in her hand while she adjusted the machine.
Following the doctor's prescribed procedure, she set
the knobs to 10 cm. of water pressure to regulate the
volume of oxygen with saline and medicine entering
the patient's lungs. She gently turned the patient's

head, noticing his flushed, puffy face and the hazy faraway look in his eyes.

"Now, Mr. Stein," she said, "we are going to place the mask over your mouth like we did a couple of hours ago, and I want you to take some deep breaths when I tell you to. You're going to feel fine, just fine."

Remy gave the man a reassuring smile and using a sterile gauze pad, she wiped the mucus that had accumulated around his mouth. She placed the mask over his nose and mouth, making sure it was held tightly on the face to prevent any leakage of precious medicinal vapors.

"Okay, Mr. Stein, let's take a deep breath now," she said encouragingly.

"Good—give me another big one."

"Again . . . Again. You're doing fine."

By the time the patient took his fifth breath, Remy was able to increase the water pressure to 15 cm. Within a few minutes, the pressure was again increased to 20 cm. The medicine that the doctor prescribed would filter in to each lung and help clear the congestion. Gradually, the patient's gasping breath become more regular and deep. Remy took another sponge from the tray and dabbed away the perspiration from the forehead of the man. As she continued to hold the mask to the patient's face, Remy turned her wrist and checked the time. She had another fifteen minutes to administer the therapy.

With the patient under control, Remy began sorting through her thoughts. She had an eerie feeling that maybe Florencio and Emil were not kidding, but why would she be acting like Teresita Basa? Why would she be so concerned with Teresita's death? She was not an intimate friend. They had talked on occasion when Remy's work extended to the morning shift. It had seemed to Remy that Teresita made a point to seek her out. By coincidence, Remy's mother and Ron Somera's father were from the same hometown. Remy had found Teresita a pleasant person to talk with. Sometimes, a mannerism or idiom of speech surfaced denoting her genteel and affluent background.

Remy noticed that a couple of times Teresita seemed over sensitive about minor infractions and would brood if someone she said hello to at the hospital did not respond. Remy had gathered Teresita really enjoyed giving and going to parties.

She had been to Teresita's apartment building once when Teresita had given a party or what she called a "blow-out" celebrating the passing of the respiratory therapy exam.

Teresita was a gracious hostess and her buffet had dishes from the various countries she had lived in and visited.

Teresita played the piano for a while and then went around spending time with each guest. When she came over to Remy, they talked for a short while and Teresita asked about her husband and family.

On other occasions at the hospital, Teresita had asked questions about Remy's marriage. They were shy, superficial questions at first but then more personal questions about the children, about her husband and how they met. One of the questions that she had asked was, "How does it feel to make

love to a man?" The surprised Remy laughed the
question off at first, but sensing that Teresita was
serious, she candidly talked about her love for her
husband.

Remy had the feeling that Teresita had wished for
the things Remy had—a loving husband and family.
She had the sad feeling that Teresita had died unful-
filled.

10

The ghetto had engulfed the surrounding neighborhood, and Franklin Park Hospital stood out as a fortress amid a forest of deteriorating buildings.

The usual activities were occurring throughout the hospital, from admitting to X-ray, to diagnostic testing and nuclear medicine, and pharmacy, then on to the indistinguishable second and third floors where the patients' rooms were located.

On the fourth floor in the surgical wing, Dr. Jose Chua stood before a row of gleaming enamel sinks preparing to assist the attending surgeon with a hernia repair. He was thinking over something that had been bothering him. He had begun to notice some change in his wife, Remy.

He knocked the water faucet with his knee, grabbed a scrub brush packet, and proceeded with the customary scrub. Dr. Chua could not identify why or when this insidious, almost immeasurable change had begun. Remy had become so temperamental. "Maybe she's working too hard," he surmised. He was concerned about her.

He knew Remy so well and for so many years.

They had met at a junior-senior high school prom. Joe was attending Ateneo, an all boys school under the guidance of Jesuit Fathers, and Remy was attending St. Paul College, an all girls high school. After high school graduation, each enrolled at the University of Santa Tomas. The university, founded in 1611, was submerged in old tradition.

The Dominican Fathers forbade the young men and women from meeting or talking, and they had segregated study areas and entered and exited from separate halls and stairways.

Joe did not know that Remy was at the large university until one Sunday afternoon at an R.O.T.C. meeting, a friend happened to mention that he had seen Remy, and she was staying at her sister's apartment in Manila on the weekends.

Obtaining the address, Joe wasted no time, and they met within a week.

They were immediately attracted to each other. At first, Joe and Remy discreetly exchanged romantic notes at a confectionary down the street from the campus with the counterlady acting as their intermediary. When Remy's family discovered their innocent encounters were growing into an intense relationship, they became alarmed. They wanted their daughter to finish college, and they strongly objected to their meetings.

Although their studies kept them busy, Joe and Remy continued their clandestine meetings. On the fifth floor of the huge university, the pharmacy and pre-med labs faced each other across the courtyard. Joe and Remy would languishingly gaze at each other, and when Joe signaled to a book he held,

Remy knew there would be a secret message tucked inside for her, and she was to pick up the book at the snack bar.

Those were exciting and daring times for the young lovers. Finally, their desire for each other could not be denied. Since Remy knew her parents would not sanction a marriage, they were secretly married by a justice of the peace. They tried to conceal their marriage, but her family found out. Tension eased when they sanctified their marriage in a traditional church ceremony two months later.

They both continued at the university for two more years. Remy received a pharmacy degree and went on to serve a clerkship in Tuquegarao while staying with Joe's mother. Joe went on to study medicine at Manila Central University. After graduating from medical school, he served a two year rotating medical residency at the Veterans Memorial Hospital in Quezon City, a suburb of Manila. He returned to his home town, Tuquegarao, in the northern section of Luzon Island, to work at Provincial Hospital.

Tuquegarao, a small commercial city nestled in a valley between two rivers is surrounded by miles of fertile green fields where farmers grow fine tobacco and rice. Life here was pleasant enough for the young professionals, but it lacked the challenge and glamour of a large city. Remy's sister, Lilly, had been working as a nurse in Chicago, and in every letter she kept extolling the opportunities in the city. Finally, Joe and Remy relented and began planning their move to the States.

The United States government has strict immigration regulations. Before allowing permanent residency and citizenship in the country, individuals had to fall within nine preference categories. By having degrees in medical fields, Joe and Remy qualified under the third category, of undermanned occupations.

After they arrived in Chicago in 1972, Remy found out, much to her dismay, that her pharmacy degree would not be accepted in the States without further schooling, two more years, something they could not afford since they now had four small girls. She heard of an on-the-job training program in respiratory therapy available at Bethesda Hospital, and she immediately took advantage of the opportunity.

As a graduate from a recognized foreign medical school, Joe had a different problem. He was required to take the test given by the Educational Council for Foreign Medical Graduates. Because of the large influx of foreign medical graduates migrating to the States, the test had become progressively harder, taking years of study before passing. Joe applied for the test and, meanwhile, landed the surgical assistant job at Franklin where he became a respected member of the hospital staff.

At Franklin, his duties consisted of assisting with surgeries in the morning and performing histories and physicals for the new admissions. He was on call every fourth night and helped in the emergency room.

Finishing the prescribed seven minute scrub, he gave his hands a shake, and holding out his arms slightly bent at the elbows, Dr. Chua headed down the corridor through the swinging doors of operating

room #1, and around the anesthesiologist at the head
of the table who was busily intubating the patient.
The waiting scrub nurse, Miss Davis, handed him a
towel and he dried his hands. She held out the sterile
gown, and he slipped into it. The circulating nurse
pulled and tied the gown from behind, and Miss
Davis held the sterile powdered gloves and he
shoved in his hands. Moving quickly to the instru-
ment table, he picked up the sheets, and with the
help of Dr. Santos, a fellow surgical technician,
draped the obese patient.

As if on cue, the surgeon walked into the room.
After the routine greetings, he was assisted with his
gown and gloves and moved to the side of the
operating table. He carefully palpated the hernia
building through the slitted opening of the blue
sheet. He looked up at the nurse and said, "Let me
have a No. 10, Davy." Miss Davis efficiently slapped
the handle of the scalpel on the surgeon's waiting
hand.

Dr. Chua drew the skin tight while the surgeon
made the opening incision into the groin. The blood
rushed profusely from the wound. The surgeon
sliced deeper, and Dr. Chua raked back the skin with
a retractor. The surgeon cut through layer after layer
of yellowish fat, stopping when needed to meticu-
lously suture the blood vessels with fine catgut or
sear the minute vessels with an electro coagulator.
The smell of singed flesh rose from the wound. He
cut through the red muscle wall criss-crossing over
the hernia. Reaching into the depth of the wound,
the intricately intertwined spermatic cord was carefully manipulated out of the way isolating the her-

nia wrapped in a sausagelike encasement. The excess hernia sack was clipped out and the defect repaired. The spermatic cord was carefully placed back in the fatty tissue. Layer by layer the structures and tissues were sutured back together. Reaching the subcutaneous skin, the surgeon said, "Joe close it up while I go dictate the case."

Before leaving the operating room, the surgeon stopped while the circulating nurse untied his gown. He peeled off his disposable gloves and gown and handed them to the nurse and pushed out the swinging doors and walked down the hall to the dictating machines.

As the other surgical assistant retracted, Dr. Chua realigned and sutured the tissue. Joe said to the nurse, "Let me have 3-0 nylon." The nurse again loaded the needle-holding forceps and placed it on the waiting hand.

The room was quiet. The only noise heard was the constant beeping of the electrocardiogram, monitoring the patient's heartbeat.

From the head of the operating table came the voice of the anesthesiologist, "How come you've been so quiet today, Joe?" and hastily added, "How much longer do you have to go?" Responding to the second question, Joe said, "Just five to ten minutes. Is everything okay there?"

"No problems. But he's so damn fat and with that short neck, I'm having some difficulty with the airway, but he's fine. I'll start bringing him out."

"Well, don't bring him out too quickly," Joe said in a kidding tone. "I don't want him to walk to the recovery room."

"No problem. You've got a big-time anesthesiologist on the case."

Joe finished closing the skin and mounded the gauze over the wound and secured the bandages. After removing his gown and gloves, he walked to the doctors' lounge.

He pulled down his paper mask and it hung at his neck. He lit a cigarette and blew the smoke into the air. He poured a cup of tar black coffee and sat down in a chair. There was no change noticeable in Joe's outward appearance as Remy began to enter his thoughts. "I can't figure this. Why is she so moody? And the way she snapped at the girls." He remembered Remy sitting at home intently watching a symphony on television and saying to their daughter, "Shut up, I'm listening to this," and then yelling toward the kitchen for her older daughter to bring her coffee from the kitchen—right away! He could not believe it was Remy. He remembered giving her a questioning look. She was never demanding. She always waited on others first. And the other day, for no apparent reason she shouted to her daughter to come home immediately from the park across the street. She had always been so patient and devoted to the children.

"Probably the overtime at the hospital and selling the house and buying the new one has been too much for her, but I thought since she had taken the real estate course, she should be the one to work with the lawyers in the negotiations," he reasoned.

"I wonder why she called Al Bascos?" he thought. "Larry Ptasinski always handled everything for us before."

He glanced at the clock on the wall. It was 9:55 a.m. It might be a good time to catch her at work. He did not want to alarm her because he usually did not call there, but he felt he needed to talk to Remy.

As he got up and walked into the doctors' dressing room, he was greeted at the door by the Director of Medical Services, Dr. Terry Winograd. He handed Joe a slip of paper and asked, "Could you do these three admissions? They are up for surgery and they have to be done right away."

Joe took the slip of paper with the patients' names and room numbers. With the other admissions coming in, he knew he had a long day ahead. He now had to concentrate on his medical duties, so he decided to postpone his talk with Remy.

11

Investigators Stachula and Epplen made their way up the litter ridden stairs of the building. The walls were splashed with graffiti, the most prominent being "Latin Kings."

The detectives were tracking a lead that they had gotten from Teresita's lawyer. The lawyer had told them about a youth who had worked for him at the time of the Basa murder. The youth had met Teresita since she had come often to his house for legal help with her citizenship papers.

"This kid," the lawyer said. "He had a mean temper . . . that's why I let him go. If I were you I would check on him."

Reaching the third floor landing, Stachula knocked hard on the door. They heard the television blaring. Stachula moved to the side of the door and Epplen moved to the other side, opening his coat and exposing his service revolver.

"Yeah, who is it?" said a rough voice from behind the door.

"Jose Rodriquez?" asked Stachula in a loud voice.

"Yeah . . . What you want, man?"

"Mr. Rodriquez . . . it's the police. We would like to talk with you." He had lowered his voice at the word police. In this area, a police officer was not a welcome sight.

"Hey man . . . What 'chu want?"

"Open the door and we'll tell you," commanded Stachula. The door opened, revealing a short, dark youth with curly black hair dressed in Levi's and a tank top shirt that accentuated his large biceps.

"What do you want?" said the youth.

"I am Investigator Stachula and this is Lee Epplen. We are investigating the murder of Teresita Basa, and we wanted to ask you some questions."

"Teresita Basa? Who the hell is she?"

"Did you ever work with Stephen Milak, an attorney?"

"Yeah, but I quit. All he wanted was a slave. Man, he was cheap!"

"Miss Basa was one of his clients. She used to go to his house," interjected Epplen.

"Oh yeah . . . She was about so tall," Rodriquez said holding up his hand to his height, "and she had black hair, and she had scars on her face from pimples or something.

"Yeah, I remember her. She was a nice lady. She was Filipino, but she could talk Spanish, you know. She had class. I often wondered why she didn't get herself a good lawyer, instead of that Mother, Milak.

"Man, that's a shame," said Rodriquez looking down and shaking his head.

Bringing up his head he asked, "When did she die?"

"On February 21st," replied Epplen.

"February 21st . . . boy, I was in the Island from the beginning of February until last week. That's the 5th of April."

"Did anyone know you were there?" asked Epplen.

"Man, everyone, my neighbors, my relatives, the travel agent. They all knew I was gone. I still owe for the ticket. You want the travel agent's number?"

"Okay, we'll take it," said Stachula. He felt the kid had a good alibi, but he would verify it.

The youth went over to the television set and grabbed a travel brochure. "Here, the number's on here."

The door slammed, and Joe turned to Lee counting down on his fingers as he said, "We've checked out her two boyfriends, we've checked everyone out at the hospital, talked to all the friends and relatives, and this is our last lead. I think we might be back to square one."

12

When Remy would drift into sleep, a troubling sensation, buried deeply, would begin to bother her. The disturbance laid tightly coiled in her subconscious. When the turbulence began, it would spin and swirl, each time getting closer. It would then recoil and disperse. As it would whirl up and sweep closer, an achromatic image began to project from its orifice, and to Remy an amorphous face was emerging. Finally, the gray funneling cloud furled again and again until from its nucleus loomed a head. It was Teresita's face.

Starting around the end of June, another menacing blackness lay convoluted in her subconscious. Even though it was more remote and dormant, it seemed threatening to Remy. It began stirring, and then lifted in a twisting convulsing surge only to return to its depths. Each time it came closer a configuration of a head began surfacing. Remy felt it might be a familiar face, but the features remained nebulous.

It was now the latter part of July and in spite of the fact Remy was physically and emotionally exhausted, she was not sleeping at all.

Now every time she closed her eyes, Teresita's face would appear with the other vaguely featured face following close behind.

Bolting up in bed, Remy's eyes veered toward the clock radio on the nightstand. The luminous dial clicked to exactly 2:30 p.m. Touching her forehead and face, she felt warm and clammy even though the room was air conditioned.

She shook trying to rid herself of the visions. She got up. Sleeping would be fruitless. Heading for the shower, she glanced in the mirror noticing her disheveled appearance.

The rest of the day was like a daze. She went through the robot motions of straightening the house and preparing dinner, and then got ready for work. She was dreading it.

As Remy got to work that evening, she said hello to Emil and stopped momentarily to talk. "You know, Emil, you're going to have to learn how to play Majong one of these days. I know a lot of people who can teach you."

"Mrs. Chua," Emil said giving her a shocked look. "Terrie always said the same thing."

"Oh, really?" she smiled, outwardly brushing off the remark. She hurried on down the hall.

Remy and her co-workers, Reynaldo Velez and Cesar Calderon, took their break around 11:45 p.m. As they went down to the cafeteria, they were joined by one of the orderlies from the inhalation therapy department, Allan Showery.

Remy went through the line, only taking coffee, and found an empty table for everyone; Reynaldo and Cesar came right behind balancing their cups of coffee on the trays.

Showery came to the table, placed the food tray down, pulled out a chair and, making himself comfortable, said, "Would anybody help me sell my townhouse?" Not getting a response, he went on, "Dr. Rivera wants to rent with an option to buy my townhouse. It's not too far from the hospital, you know. It's got a fireplace in every room."

As Showery went on describing the townhouse, Remy wondered how someone on an orderly's salary could afford a townhouse, particularly one in the fairly high rent district around the hospital. She caught Reynaldo's eyes and nudged him with her elbow as if to say, "Where would he get the money to buy a townhouse around here?"

Reynaldo smiled and rolled up his eyes in an exasperated look. He had gotten Remy's message.

Showery continued talking, "That patient they brought in, Freddie Tanaca, the one with the stab wound near the heart. He has pleural effusion and they have him in the coronary unit. I know who he is! You should see him perform those karate moves. He is so fast . . . Like this!" Showery's sinewy dark arms moved rapidly, mimicking a karate chop. "If he makes it through, you people better watch it. I heard he's after your hide."

The two other men seemed oblivious to the comment, but to Remy it registered as a disguised warning, and she responded, "Why should this Tanaca want to get our hide? His mother is one of our people."

The subject was dropped.

As soon as Showery left, the conversation turned to Tagalog, their national language in the Philippines.

"Boy, that man sure likes to brag," said Reynaldo.

"Yeah, he sure does," added Cesar. "I'm sure that he is just renting that place. There is no way he could afford to buy a townhouse in this area. No way! And have you heard the one about the plane he says he keeps at Meigs Field, so he can fly to New York on weekends to lecture?" Everyone nodded their heads in agreement.

Remy asked, "How's his friend, Ely, our fine supervisor? It makes me mad everytime I think how he treated the late Teresita. Did I tell you that he wouldn't even let her have time off to study for her respiratory exams, and he let the other girl off? Teresita passed her exam anyway, but the other girl didn't."

"I had heard that they had some disagreements," said Reynaldo.

The small group got up from the table, taking their trays and placing them in the special rack that stood by the elevator door. As Cesar pressed the button, Remy leaned against the wall waiting for the elevator to arrive.

Returning to the inhalation therapy department, Remy checked her assignment and was annoyed when she saw that she had been assigned to a case in the coronary unit. It was a difficult case. The patient had been stabbed near the heart, and he required inhalation therapy for twenty minutes, every hour on the hour. Remy knew she was in for a long night.

Checking the supplies in her cart, she noticed that

she was missing an oxygen mask. She looked up and saw the orderly, Showery, across the large room.

"Al!" called Remy. Showery looked at her.

"Al, I need an oxygen mask. Could you please get one for me?" As Showery left the room, Remy's attention turned back to checking the orders on the clipboard.

"Hum," she thought to herself. "This patient is Tanaca. He's the one we were talking about."

Remy was lost in concentration when from the corner of her eye she saw an arm reach from behind her.

In that fraction of a second that it took her eyes to perceive the quick movement, her mind flashed an intense vision. It was as if somehow she were looking at herself from afar, only it was not her. Someone was reaching for the person in her vision with evil intent.

Remy reeled around, gasping, almost dropping the patient's clipboard.

"Here's your oxygen mask, Mrs. Chua," said Allan Showery. He was smiling, but when he saw the terrified look on Remy's face, his smile vanished. Remy grabbed the mask out of Showery's hand, and swiftly wheeled her inhalation therapy machine out of the room to the elevator.

Remy took the elevator down to the coronary unit. As she approached the nurses' station, a male nurse said, "I don't know why we have to bother so much with patients like that. He is almost dead."

"Well, we'll have to give it a try, anyhow," answered Remy as she headed towards the patient's room. When she entered the room, Remy understood what the man had meant. The patient was indeed almost dead. His pupils were dilated and his breathing was strained and sporadic.

Remy set up her machine and administered the treatment. She continued the treatments every hour on the hour for the rest of the night. By early morning, the patient had coughed up a great deal of secretions from his congested lungs and his breathing seemed easier. Remy was exhausted, but she felt that she had helped make the patient more comfortable, at least for that night.

She returned to the respiratory therapy main room, and found Showery cleaning the equipment and preparing the machines. He was obviously behind in his work and when he spotted Remy, he said, "How about giving me a hand cleaning up some of this equipment?"

A strange sensation took hold of Remy when she looked at Showery. There was a swirling and spinning mirage as the man's dark face seemed to surge at her. Suddenly the mirage came into focus and Remy realized at once why the nebulous image in her vision had been so familiar. The face was Showery's. When Remy opened her mouth to answer, the voice was cold and harsh, *"No, that is your job! I have my job. I am a therapist, and you are only an orderly."*

Showery seemed startled by the sound of her voice and the intensity of her stare. He cajoled, "Why is it that you hate me so much, Mrs. Chua?"

Remy's voice returned to her normal tone and she took a deep breath and answered, "I don't hate you

Al! Really, I don't hate you." With that, she turned and walked out of the room.

Outside in the corridor, Remy saw Jennie Prince and hurried over to her. Grabbing her by the arm, Remy whispered, "Jennie, I am frightened by that man Showery."

"You know, Remy, I am afraid also," and she added in a low voice, "I think he is after me. Naty, the girl who took Teresita's place, quit because he had been making advances to her."

As she was talking, Jennie glanced over Remy's shoulder and noticed that the respiratory therapy department door was slightly ajar. Since the door had an automatic return, someone must have been holding it open.

"Listen, we can't talk here." Then motioning with her head and eyes toward the door, "The walls have ears. Call me when you get home, Remy."

By the time Remy finished her assignments for the morning and quitting time came, she was so nervous she was afraid to go to her car. She hesitated at the door and mentally pictured where she had parked her car. She pulled out her keys from her purse and ran to the parking lot. Once inside, she checked all the door locks and started the ignition.

During her drive home she kept seeing the faces of Teresita and Showery flashing before her.

When she arrived home, only her older daughter was there. The other children were playing in the nearby park. Remy sent her daughter to bring the other girls home. She gave the message she wanted them home, immediately! While the daughter ran after her sisters, Remy hurried around the house locking all the windows and turning on all the lights.

When the girls came back, she gave strict orders that they had to stay home. She absolutely did not want them outside. Remy then went into the kitchen and using the wall phone she nervously dialed Jennie's number.

"Jennie, I am glad that you talked to me about Showery. There is something about that man that really frightens me."

"I know what you mean," answered Jennie, "and we aren't the only ones. I was talking with Rudy the other night and he said that he remembered Teresita telling him that she could not watch television because the set was broken and that Showery was coming to fix it."

"Oh, don't tell me that Jennie. Now I'm really afraid." She paused, and then said, "Listen Jennie, I haven't been feeling too well lately and I need a few days off. Do you think that it will be okay?"

"I don't know, Remy. It's fine with me, but it's up to the daytime supervisor and you know how short-handed we are. That's one of the reasons you have been able to accumulate all that overtime. Anyhow, I'll see what I can do, but I can't promise you anything."

Remy thanked Jennie and hung up the phone. As she was walking out of the kitchen, the phone rang. She turned and picked up the receiver on the second ring.

"Hello . . . hello," said Remy, but the line was dead. She was not concerned about the call as she hung up the phone.

When she walked into the large living room where her girls were watching television, the younger daughter gave her a message, "Daddy said that he has to attend a meeting tonight and that he will be late."

"That's all right honey," said Remy and trying to present a calm exterior she gently touched the side of the girl's face. "I'm not working tonight, so I'll be here."

When Joe Chua drove into his driveway, he was surprised to see all of the lights in the house on. They seemed to brighten the entire block. It was a little past eleven on the dashboard clock.

He inserted his key in the lock and pushed open the door. Again to his surprise in the middle of the living room were all the girls and Remy huddled under blankets on the floor watching television.

"What is this, a pajama party?" asked Joe good-humoredly. But when he looked once more at Remy, the humor was gone. His wife was wearing her old worn bathrobe, her face was flushed and her eyes were puffy with dark circles.

"Remy, what's going on?" he said irritably.

"Joe," Remy said breathlessly as she pulled him toward the kitchen. "At work, there is a man who frightens me."

"Frightens you? What do you mean?"

"Joe, I haven't been sleeping well. Every time I close my eyes, I have like nightmares. I see faces. One belongs to the man I am telling you about. You know the one I mentioned before that brags about how great he is at karate and tells the stories about his Viet Nam days."

"But has the man threatened you or said anything, Remy?"

"No, no. He hasn't said anything. It's just this feeling I get. I am afraid."

Joe was about to respond to Remy when the phone rang. He picked it up.

"Hello? . . . who? James Simcus? No, there is no one here by that name. What number are you dialing? That's the right number, but there is no one here by that name. Sorry."

As Joe hung up the phone, Remy said, "I had a number of calls today and it is always the same thing. There is no one on the line."

Joe grabbed his wife by the shoulders and gave her a gentle shake. He looked down into her eyes. "Remy, no one is trying to hurt you. There is nothing to worry about. You have just been working too hard. You need rest."

With his hand, he lifted her chin and gently kissed her lips. He put his arm around Remy's shoulders and walked her to the bedroom.

13

By seven a.m. the next morning, Joe had left the house, as usual, for the hospital.

Remy was sitting at the kitchen table. A clouded gaze was fixed in her eyes as she stared into space. She had not slept at all.

Last night, when Joe had put her to bed, she tried falling asleep. Sleep eluded her again. As soon as her eyes closed, the faces of Teresita and Showery flashed through her mind, and one more thing, the smell of smoke had filtered into her nostrils.

She had pretended to be sleeping when Joe had come to bed because she had not wanted to worry him. He had been studying for his boards until about two in the morning.

As she lay in bed, the smell of smoke had been so real that several times she had almost screamed. Fortunately, she collected her senses before she made any sound.

When she had moved closer to Joe seeking comfort from his calm exterior, the light from the moon passed through the window, casting a dim shadow over his face. It did not look like Joe. His face had transformed into that of an old wrinkled man with a tear in the crevice of his eye. His lips began moving and out came a strained throaty whisper, "Un peso, un peso." The old man was begging for a peso. She pushed herself away from him and tried to get out of bed, but Joe's face returned to normal. He had been sleeping. She knew it was something wrong with her, and she lay back down in bed.

Now Remy got up from her chair and began pacing back and forth in her small kitchen. She was confused. She was usually composed with good judgment and here she was pacing like a frightened caged animal. The visions were unlike anything she had ever experienced, and the smell of smoke was real, very real.

Remy abruptly stopped her pacing and frustratedly rubbed her upper arms with her hands.

"Dios Mio," she said aloud. "I have to get out of this mood."

No sooner had the words passed her lips when Remy stopped and her mouth flung open. "My God, what's happening to me? That isn't the way I talk. What's going on?" Remy was almost in tears as she reached for the phone and dialed. The girls were still asleep, and she did not want to frighten them. She was calling her mother. "Nanang, Mother, please come. I am so afraid! I need you Nanang, I need help!"

Remy's mother, Guillerma, was very alarmed, but soothed her daughter with a confident facade saying, "Don't worry, dear, your father and I will be there in a few minutes."

Guillerma nervously placed the receiver down

and with a sense of urgency called out to her husband, Vicente. "Papang, we've got to go to Remy's. There is something wrong."

They too had become concerned by the noticeable changes in their daughter. In his letters to the relatives back home in the Philippines, Vicente had urged that they pray for Remy's health. She seemed so irritable and morose. The last time they had been with her she looked drawn.

The parents hurried over to Remy's and were there in less than a half hour. Guillerma made Remy strong tea and helped her to bed while Vicente called Joe. The operator at Franklin Park Hospital told him that the doctor was in surgery but she would leave a message for him.

It was noon by the time Joe returned the call. "What's up?" he asked when Vicente answered. As Vicente explained what had been happening, Joe anxiously said, "Papang, I'll get there as quickly as possible and I'll bring a sedative for Remy."

He wasted no time and spoke with the medical service chief, Dr. Winograd, hurriedly explaining Remy's problem and asking if he could leave early. Dr. Winograd said very sympathetically, "It shouldn't be a problem, Joe, just have one of the other residents cover for you. Let me know how your wife is doing."

After telling one of his fellow surgical technicians he had to leave, Joe changed clothes and hurried to the pharmacy downstairs. He picked up a dozen capsules of Sinequan, 50 mg., a strong psychotherapeutic sedative, from the pharmacist.

It was almost two o'clock when Joe got home.

When he entered the bedroom, he was shocked to see the condition Remy was in. She was sitting in bed with her back propped against the headboard. She gripped the old yellow bathrobe tightly around her and her hair was matted against her head. Her dark hollow eyes saw Joe but she made no response. Joe said nothing either. He went to the kitchen and came back to the bedroom with a glass of water and the Sinequan capsule. Remy never relied on medication, but this time she took the medication dutifully. Her mother made her get under the sheets and placed a pillow under Remy's head, trying to console her.

A half an hour later, the strong sedative had taken effect and for the first time in days Remy was sleeping peacefully.

Joe and his inlaws returned to the kitchen and talked for a long time. He tried to appease Papang and Nanang by explaining that Remy was merely exhausted. It was the hard work at the hospital and at home, plus the added tension of moving to the new house. Joe told all those things to his inlaws, but he really did not believe them.

Nanang made coffee and Joe went to the bedroom to check on Remy. She was sound asleep. A smile crossed his handsome face as he gazed down at his wife. It was a relief to see her lying there so peacefully.

As Joe returned to the kitchen to report the good news to Guillerma and Vicente, he glanced down the hallway into the living room where the younger girls were busy playing and the older girls were watching television. Everything was calming down.

Remy's parents were pleased to hear that their daughter was finally resting. Joe checked his watch and tapped it. It was 5:30, and Remy had been sleeping over three hours. He remembered that he had to call his lawyer, Al Bascos, to find out when they were to take possession of the house. Since Bascos usually stayed in his office until 6:00, Joe knew he had just enough time. He picked up the phone and dialed the number and on the third ring a pleasant woman's voice answered, and Joe said, "This is Dr. Chua. May I please speak to Mr. Bascos?"

While Joe waited for the lawyer, he stepped outside the kitchen and looked down the hallway and into his bedroom where he could clearly see Remy lying in bed. Her figure was illuminated by the iridescent afternoon sun rays streaming through the window. "What a beautiful sight," Joe thought.

The voice on the phone was loud and clear. "How are you doing, Joe?"

"Al!" Joe answered cheerfully. The vision of his wife resting peacefully was still vividly etched in his mind as he turned back into the kitchen. He held the phone to his ear and pulled the trailing cord. "Al, it's nice to talk to you." That was all Joe was able to say to the attorney.

The next thing he heard was a blood curdling scream, emanating from Remy's room.

14

In the bedroom Remy was asleep when Joe spoke out the name Al. The sound of the name penetrated through the gossamery curtain of Remy's sleep, setting up an ephemeral chain of events. Suddenly, Remy felt her body being transported to a deep dark grave. She could distinctly hear "Al" rebounding from the dark walls of the grave.

Al . . . Al . . . AL . . . AL . . . AL . . . Al . . . Al . . . AL . . . AL . . . AL . . .

Remy felt a deep stirring within her and darkness enveloped her. She was smothering. A scream poured from her lungs. "Ayiii! Ayiii!!"

Joe was startled when he heard the blood curdling scream from Remy's room. Before he could react, Nanang was running down the hall to Remy with Papang close behind.

As Nanang rushed into the room, the unearthly atmosphere made her stop dead in her tracks. The room felt cold and damp and the air felt electrified, darting and deflecting off the walls. The stormy currents riveted through Nanang's body and the hair on her head literally stood up on end.

Papang gasped as he saw what was happening to his wife, but he did not stare long. Something else demanded his immediate attention. Walking towards them with closed eyes and outstretched arms was Remy. She was screaming and babbling in a language that sounded like Spanish.

"¡Mi Mama, Ayuda . . . Ayuda! Ayiii!"

Remy's face was red. The veins on the sides of her neck dilated with the force of her screams.

"Mama! Mama! Ayiii!"

When Remy flung her arms high over her head, her open bathrobe flailed like a cape. Her chest heaved from the exertion. Suddenly, as if she were a helpless puppet on a string, she was jerked onto the bed. Her body was rigid and her feet stuck straight out over the edge of the mattress.

Nanang and Papang scurried to Remy. They tried to reposition her farther up on the bed, but together they could not move her small frame. Vicente, a tall strong man, tried again but could not budge his daughter's body on the bed.

"Joe, Joe," they called in unison.

The moment Joe Chua walked into the bedroom the chill and heavyness about the air radiated an aura of impending danger. The appropriate brain cells instantly assimilated the subliminal message triggering a primal response which made the hair on the back of his neck stand at attention.

Remy's parents, their mesmerized gaze reflecting intense fright, stood to one side of the bed looking down at their daughter's supine form.

Joe cautiously approached the low bed and kneeled down beside it, trying to reason out the situation. As an experienced physician, he knew instinctively what to look for when dealing with an unconscious person. Remy's eyes were closed and he noted that, other than her face being flushed, her skin color appeared normal. His next move was to check for radial pulse. Her arms were wedged close to her body. He expertly felt her wrist. When he tried to lay her arm in a better position to check again, he could not move it. He let go instantly and nervously brought his fingers through his thick black hair, pushing it back from his worried brow.

Joe went on to ask the often asked question of a fainting victim: "How do you feel?" But, for some unexplainable reason, the question came out, "Who are you?"

Remy's body stirred slightly and her mouth began to move.

"I am Teresita Basa!" The Voice was strong and vibrant. Chills went up and down Joe's spine. It was not Remy's voice, of that Joe was certain.

Joe swallowed hard, and it took him a moment to respond. When he did answer, his voice was barely audible, almost trembling. "What . . . What is your purpose in coming here?"

"Dr. Chua, I would like to ask for help from you," said the Voice.

"What kind of help do you want from me?" asked Joe as he gestured back to himself with his hand.

The Voice sounded louder and somewhat disturbed. *"Up to this time nothing has been done in regards to the man who killed me."*

For a second Joe thought that his ears were playing tricks. The words, "Killed Me," ricocheted in and about his brain. Joe looked around the room. Nanang and Papang were standing like statues. They had not moved since the Voice had begun speaking. Looking over his shoulder, Joe saw two of his daughters standing in the doorway. Their eyes were open wide in disbelief for they too had heard the words.

"I don't see how I can help you," Joe began haltingly, "I have not met you before, and . . ."

"Well, I know you," the Voice interrupted sharply, *"and Vicente and Guillerma and the girls."*

"I still don't see how I can help, Teresita . . ." Joe had surprised himself, wondering why he had used the name Teresita. After a moment, he went on, "It would seem to me that this is a police matter. I can not do anything."

Remy's face reddened, and the veins on her neck began bulging again. This time the Voice of Teresita became insistent, twinged with a trace of indolent anger. *"You have to help me! Tell the police. They will believe you. You are a physician."*

Joe became worried. He did not want any harm befalling Remy and thought reasoning with the Voice might be the best approach. "What do you want me to tell the police?"

The Voice hesitated for a few seconds before it answered. When it did, it was softer and feminine, almost secretive. *"A man came into my apartment. He choked me and then . . . and then he stabbed me and . . ."* The Voice was almost sobbing. Remy's head rose from the pillow and the enraged voice shouted, *"Ayiii! ¡Mama! ¡Mama Ayudame por favor, Ayudame!"*

Joe's heart skipped a beat. The Voice was speaking

Spanish. Remy spoke no Spanish. Being from the Luzon region of the Philippines, the Chuas spoke that area's dialect, Ilocano, as well as Tagalog. They did not speak Spanish.

"Teresita, I want to help you, but I do not know how," implored Joe. "I just can't go to the police and tell them that you have told me. They won't believe me."

"Tell them, Dr. Chua! Tell them!" Remy's body shook as Teresita's voice resounded from the depths of her chest.

Suddenly, the pressure of the air in the room seemed normal as if a magnetic force had lifted. Reaching for Remy's hands, Joe was able to lift and hold them in his hands.

Teresita had left.

"Nanang, Nanang." It was Remy speaking and her eyes were wide open looking at her parents. "I am so cold"—as she crossed her arms against her body—"and thirsty."

Joe lifted Remy and easily repositioned her on the bed. He gently placed a pillow under Remy's head and quickly covered her with a blanket. He ran his hand over her forehead and hair. Her usually full and soft hair felt dry and brittle to his touch.

Guillerma was back with a large glass of water. When Joe helped Remy drink, he noticed how pale and dessicated her lips were. Remy asked weakly, "What happened to me? Joe . . . ? Nanang? What happened?"

"Don't worry about it now honey. Try and get some rest. We'll talk about it later," Joe said and then added reassuringly, "We will all be here with you. Go to sleep now."

Remy dropped her head on the soft pillow, totally exhausted from her experience, and she was asleep in a moment.

"NALUGANAN."

"What . . . ?" asked Joe, looking up at his father-in-law. Vicente was standing rooted to the same spot that he had been in when the Voice was speaking.

"Naluganan!" repeated Vicente. "Remy was possessed by the spirit of the dead woman." Vicente appeared drained, but inside, he had a strong determination and purpose, and was resolved to do something about the spirit that had possessed his daughter. He would be ready if there was a next time.

"Possessed?" thought Joe, the word stuck in his mind. Possessions were something out of old folk tales. They were not supposed to happen in the nineteen seventies, in the middle of one of the world's largest metropolises. It can not be happening.

Yet, Joe had heard the Voice. Its eerie timbre and hollowness brought a shiver to him. There was no question in his mind that it was not Remy talking. He knew he would have to get medical advice.

15

"Let's raise it five cents." All the participants nodded their heads in agreement. The winner of the previous game threw the dice on the cloth covered card table and the game opened. The small cubes flipped and rolled and lapped over to a stop. The spots facing up totaled seven. There was a murmur of excitement from the four players. Seven meant the betting was doubled. Five or nine would have doubled it, also. They silently counted clockwise around the table to seven. That player drew seventeen of the 144 two-toned orange and white plastic cubes from the three diagonal rows placed in the middle of the table. The other players drew sixteen.

The plastic cubes, thicker than dominos, were marked with numbers from one to nine and symbols with multi-colored sticks, flowers, interlocking balls, and Chinese characters which the players tried to match in consecutive suits. The players picked extra cubes from the center pile or threw back what they did not want. The players' motions were in such rapid sequence, they seemed to be moving in unison. Before long, one of the players slapped the cubes down on the table. She had won the game. Each player paid out their amount. All the cubes were pushed to the center of the table to be shuffled and arranged for the next game.

"So that's how you play Majong," said Dr. Friedmann who had been standing behind Joe Chua and watching the game. "It's like gin rummy. By the way, where is your wife today, Joe?"

"She stayed home today," said Joe, and then jokingly added, "She says that one gambler in the family is enough." Everyone laughed.

The hostess came into the room and told everyone that the food was ready. They all got up and moved to the dining room where the long table was spread with typical Philippine cuisine.

"Okay, Dr. Friedmann," said the hostess as she guided him to the table, "let me explain what everything is. This is Igado, chopped liver and pork, and this is Pinakbet, which has green beans, okra, and eggplant. Our food is usually flavored with soy sauce and we always serve everything with rice. And for dessert we have Bibingca, which is a pudding thickened with rice flour and flavored with coconut."

Dr. Chua put some of the food on his plate, but he was not interested in eating. The main reason he had come tonight was to talk to John Friedmann. He did not know exactly how to approach him with Remy's problem, but he was hoping John could give him some advice.

As he followed Dr. Friedmann into the large living room, Joe asked, "Mind if I join you, John?"

"Not at all, let's sit here." They sat down on the long L-shaped couch.

"John, I ran into a very interesting case. This patient, . . ." started Dr. Chua carefully, "it's a woman who says she is possessed by the spirit of a dead woman. A woman who was murdered six months ago."

"So what else is new?" said John as he laid his fork down on his plate.

"Right now, in our psychiatric department, we have two Jesus Christs, one of them is a woman. Maybe, that should tell you something about women's liberation." He went on: "And there's one fellow who says he's from the planet Krypton, he talks a foreign language, Rock and Roll, and he strums an imaginary guitar and yelps to high heaven. He must have thought he was Superman or the Six Million Dollar Man because he jumped from a three story building and busted the hell out of his ankle. Amazing his injuries weren't more serious or even fatal."

"Well, this woman is not that way at all, she doesn't think she is the dead woman, she . . ." Before Joe could finish his sentence, John went on.

"Joe, they all look like they are normal, and in their minds, they actually believe their manifestations are real."

"But, couldn't there really be a true case of possession? You have to admit we don't understand everything that happens. Surely, there must be some foundation to all those stories that we hear from time to time," said Joe prodding for an answer.

John gave Joe a disgusted look and shook his head

back and forth impatiently. "Joe, Joe . . . those stories are all talk. Two years ago, we had a man who claimed he was possessed by the devil. One of the residents really wanted to help him. You know how altruistic residents are. He went to the medical library and agonizingly researched all the medical literature and you know what he found?"

John answered his own question, "Nothing, nothing at all. You look under possession in a medical library, and the only thing they discuss are possessive mothers! The people that claim to have been possessed by some spirit have never been medically scrutinized. There is just no documentation." John was getting up now. "Show me a case where there was a trained medical observer present at a so-called 'supernatural experience,' and then you might have something."

Joe Chua opened his mouth to reply, but before he could get a word out, the hostess was saying, "All right you two, no more shop talk. Let's get back in there and teach John how to play Majong. Joe, your playing partners are waiting for you at the table."

Joe smiled half heartedly and followed the doctor into the game room. Joe's hopes sank to disappointment. He had wanted to talk to someone about Remy. At least, he had gotten some information, and if Teresita ever visited again, he was determined to conduct himself as a competent physician and observer and not as an alarmed eyewitness.

16

Two days had passed since the Voice of Teresita had spoken through Remy. Vicente and Guillerma were still staying with the Chuas. The girls had continued to sleep in the living room. The closeness of the family provided security.

There was some semblance of normalcy in the Chua household, but beneath the thin veneer of normalcy was a lingering apprehension that Teresita would visit again.

Remy's disturbing visions had been absent since her possession, and she had actually been able to sleep. She was up and around the house talking with Joe, her parents, and the children. They talked about life in the Philippines and her student days. They talked about the children and their schools. They tried to avoid talking about Teresita, but everytime there was a pause in the conversation, her name came up.

The conversation finally got around to their new home in Skokie, and Remy suddenly realized that they still did not know the exact day that they could move into the house.

"The sooner we get out of here," thought Remy, "the better it will be for all of us."

She would call their lawyer. On the kitchen counter, she flipped open her personal directory to "B," found Al Bascos' name, and dialed his number.

The line went dead.

Shaking the receiver, Remy waited until she heard the dial tone and commenced dialing the number again, making sure that she was reading it correctly. After a few moments, the line went dead once more.

Chagrined at the malfunctioning telephone, Remy tapped furiously at the button on the phone cradle until she heard the dial tone. "Look, I'm dialing right," she said impatiently while pointing at the number in the book. Her mother was watching.

She began saying each number out loud as she dialed, "Seven . . . Seven . . . Two . . ."

Remy felt a dull pain centered in her breastbone. The pain quickly intensified, and she had to let go of the telephone receiver. Thrusting up her arms, she clutched her chest. Her body began contorting from the excruciating pain penetrating her sternum and she gasped forcing air out of her lungs.

As the pain eased, Remy felt her body slowly floating up in a vacuum. Then a curious and distinct heaviness pushed down from her shoulders as if someone were stepping into her body. The heavy sensation slowly slithered through her.

Guillerma rushed over to Remy and supported her.

"Nanang," she said softly to her mother, "Terrie is here again."

Guillerma put her arm around Remy's waist and

gradually started walking her to the bedroom. She had the definite feeling that the person she was accompanying was not her daughter, but a stranger encompassed by her daughter's form.

Vicente had come in from the outside at about the same time that Guillerma was leading Remy to the bedroom. He instinctively knew that the dead woman had invaded his daughter's body again. He quickly went to the bedroom that he and Guillerma were using and reached for the paper bag he had hidden underneath the bed, and from it pulled out a black cloth. He hurried to the closet, shoved over some clothes, and grabbed the long switch tilted in the corner. The day before, he had gone out to the yard and cut the long branch from a lilac bush. He had cleaned off the twigs except for the ones at the end. With a snap of his wrist, he tested the Latigo.

He was going to help Remy!

By the time he entered Remy's room, Nanang was making Remy comfortable in bed. Vicente handed his wife one end of the cloth, and together they laid it on Remy so that only her shoulders and face were exposed. They noticed a rattling sound in her breathing.

Vicente was going to drive away whatever was possessing his daughter, and shaking his fist in a determined gesture he said to himself, "I'll drive you out!"

Vicente had to look for Joe and left the room. Joe was sitting at the dining room table studying. As he reviewed his notes, he would stop occasionally to underline with a black marker. He was unaware of what was happening to Remy.

Looking down at Joe, Papang said simply, "Joe, we have a visitor."

Joe understood immediately.

He pushed his chair away from the table and stood up. He combed his hair back with his fingers and pushed his shirt into the waist of his pants. He resolutely walked towards the bedroom, gathering his thoughts as he did.

"*Dr. Chua*," said the Voice as Joe entered the room. Joe was momentarily taken back, both by the sight of his wife covered with the black sheet and the commanding resonance of the Voice.

"*Dr. Chua*," repeated the Voice, "*did you talk to the police?*"

"No, I did not," said Joe as he bravely sat at the foot of the bed.

"*You did not! Why not? I told you that you had to call the police.*" The Voice was sharp and angry.

"I told you before that I just couldn't go to the police without proof."

"*Proof? What kind of proof do you need? I already told you that I was killed.*"

"Yes, but you did not tell me how and by whom." Joe was beginning to get a hold of himself. He was thinking clearly now.

"*I told you that Al killed me!*" The Voice spoke with such intensity that the force could be felt throughout the room.

"*Allan, he killed me! He killed me! Ayiii, animal!*"

Joe tried to get the attention of the Voice again. He wanted to ask more questions. "Please Teresita, tell me how it happened."

"I let Al in the apartment, and he killed me."

"But why did you let him in?" asked Joe incredulously.

"Al was a friend of mine from the hospital." The Voice was quieter now. *"I let him into my apartment . . ."*

"And what happened?" asked Joe encouragingly, looking intently at Remy's perspiring face. Before the Voice answered, there was a snapping noise above his head. Crack!! . . . Crack!!!

Joe recoiled and looking up saw Vicente's anxious face. He was shaking the long stick.

"Get out from my daughter if you are evil . . . Get out spirit . . . Get out!" Vicente started chanting. He moved back and forth around the foot of the bed.

Crack . . . ! Crack . . . ! Crack . . . !

Vicente moved closer to the head of the bed and with a loud snap, hit near the pillow and proceeded with his chant, "Get out, get out woman! Go away. Out with you!" Vicente's hand was poised above his head with the stick ready to descend on the bed when the Voice shouted,

"Get away, old man!"

Vicente's arm remained raised in midair, as if held by a force.

"You can't drive me away!" The Voice was so penetrating that Vicente obediently heeded the order and stepped back.

"Dr. Chua, you tell the police. Did you hear! Tell them!" The command from the Voice was implicit.

The tension in the room slowly dissipated, and Joe realized that Teresita was gone.

Guillerma, who had been pacing outside in the hallway, realized Teresita had left and came back into the room. It was too upsetting for her to watch her daughter's ordeal.

"Remy," said Joe shaking his wife's arm.

Remy's eyes opened slowly and focused on her husband's face. She tried getting up.

"Stay down," said Joe as he gently pushed her shoulders back and asked, "Are you thirsty?"

Remy gave him an affirmative nod, and Nanang, taking her cue, went for the water.

When Guillerma returned with the water, Joe and Vicente were off towards the corner of the room talking in low whispers.

"What are we going to do, Joe? Are you going to tell the police?"

Joe pulled a cigarette from the pack in his shirt pocket and lit it. Letting out the first puff of smoke, he looked at his hands and realized they were steady. "Like a rock," he thought. Teresita had come and he had handled it. He knew he had been part of a psychic experience, but this time he was not scared. Turning to Papang, he finally answered. "I don't know what I am going to do, but I can't go to the police. They'll think we're crazy."

Guillerma was sitting down on the bed next to her daughter, and Remy was saying, "I want to see a priest, Nanang."

"We'll go to church tomorrow," said Guillerma trying to comfort her. "I'll call Father Aquino."

"No, Nanang, I don't want to see him again. You

know what he told me yesterday. He said to let Teresita rest in peace. I've got to go to someone else." She thought for a moment, and then added, "There is an old church that I've seen on the way to work . . . I'll go there tomorrow."

17

It was late evening of what had been a typically hot July day. The blades of the fan sluggishly rotated the heavy air around the large dark panelled study of the church rectory. Sitting at the massive oak desk and wearing a short sleeved black shirt with a stiff white collar encircling the neck was the pastor. He pulled uncomfortably at his collar. His snowy white crew cut hair emphasized his bright ruddy face and steel blue eyes behind thick wire framed glasses.

Father Francis J. Cummings had been with the church for five years. The church, located on the north side of Chicago, was in what city hall classified as a marginal neighborhood. The Polish and German communities had been dwindling away for the last fifteen years and were being replaced by Spanish, Appalachian white, and some Asians. Some of the old congregation remained in the neighborhood, but they were dying off.

When Father Cummings came to the parish in 1972, the parish school was at the point of closing, but tightening the budget and hard work had kept the school open. And now with the school year only six weeks away, he had a great deal of work to do. He felt that with God's help, the school would be financially stable in a couple of years and he could then retire with a sense of substantial accomplishment.

He had a special affection for the children in his school. He felt needed. The children were mostly Spanish now, and Father Cummings was able to communicate fluently in their language which was helpful in dealing with their parents. His ability to speak the language had improved greatly these last three years.

He thought of the priest who had taught him Spanish, Father Augustin Martinez. "It's ironic why Augustin should come to mind," he mused.

His thoughts began circulating, like a pond of water in which a pebble has been thrown, rippling and wavering into expanding circles until they reach the shore.

One thought that had been circulating in the periphery of his mind was of the pleasant Filipino woman who had come to him for advice earlier that day. She had become extremely distressed as she tried to explain to him that her body had been possessed by the spirit of a woman who had been murdered. She was frightened by this phenomenon and pleaded with the priest for help and comfort.

He doubted that he had comforted her when he explained she should not be concerned and that he would pray for her. He probably was more abrupt than he had meant to be. There were too many things that required his attention. "Was it really that?" he thought.

The tired priest leaned his elbows on the desk and tilted the lamp out of the way. He pulled off his glasses and gently dropped them on the desk piled with letters and bills. With his thumb and index finger, he massaged the bridge of his bulbous nose.

His thoughts began circulating counterclockwise, back many years to his assignment in Central America as a young priest. He had been sent by the Archbishop to spend one year in a small town to help the local parish priest and to learn Spanish. The older priest to whom he had been assigned was Father Martinez. While the town was small, it served a large surrounding area.

Most of the campesinos, farmers, were too busy eking out a living from their minute plots of land to be able to come to church every Sunday. When they did come, it was for festive occasions, the Three Kings days during the Christmas holidays, and Holy Week, or for baptisms, weddings, and funerals.

He remembered the night toward the end of his assignment when a group of impatient campesinos from a nearby village had pushed their way into the dining room of the rectory and how the housekeeper had argued with the campesinos and tried to prevent them from interrupting the dinner of the two priests.

Father Martinez, unperturbed by all the commotion, pushed his chair away from the long wooden table and with his linen napkin still in his hand walked over to the men. He apparently knew the thin dark mustached man who politely bowed and nervously rolled the brim of the straw hat that he held in his hands.

"¿Que pasa, mi amigo?" asked Father Martinez.

"¡Padre Martinez, por favor, yo deseo ayuda."

"¡Es mi hija. La pobrecita esta poceida por un demonio!"

Father Cummings, watching the animated conversation, knew enough Spanish to understand what the distraught farmer was saying. The man wanted Father Martinez to help his daughter who was possessed by a demon.

Father Martinez handed the napkin to the housekeeper and walked to the foyer and picked up his Bible, stole, and hat. He stepped outside into the churchyard and moved toward his jeep as the entourage of excited campesinos followed.

The next day Father Martinez had sent word back to the rectory that he would be away for a few days. He returned seven days later in the middle of the night and went straight to bed. He slept for two days. Father Cummings was astonished when he saw the priest. Father Martinez had aged drastically in those seven days.

A month passed before he mentioned anything about his mysterious seven day ordeal. The two priests were having an after-dinner sherry when Father Martinez said, "Francis, it was a battle. I met our old enemy. I fought him all those days. I was scared . . . really scared, but we won." The kindly old priest sipped gently from the glass, savoring the liquid, and continued, "I don't think I would have the strength to do it again. I'm too old to battle any more demons, Francis, too old."

Father Cummings' eyes began to focus again as he roused from his reverie. He looked at the pile of work on his desk, bills to pay, letters to answer, book orders to approve, and some teacher contracts to review.

He wanted to help the woman, but he did not have the time, and besides he was too old, and there was too much to do for the church and the school.

He would say a prayer for her. He reverently bowed his white head and prayed.

"Heavenly Father . . ."

18

. . . THE WOUNDS UPON THY SHOULDER MADE BY
THE HEAVY CROSS THOU DIDST CARRY. ITS WEIGHT
TORE THY FLESH AND BARED THY SHOULDER BONE,
WHICH CAUSED THEE SUFFERINGS MORE THAN DID
THY OTHER WOUNDS . . .

Remy drew her fingers under each line and silently recited the passage from the cream colored
prayer book she held in her hand and gripped beneath it a small silver crucifix.

She was sitting on the passenger side of the car as
Joe drove to Edgewater Hospital.

Remy had called the hospital earlier that Saturday
morning to ask if she could pick up her check. Joe
insisted on accompanying her because he knew she
was too frightened to go alone, but he had wanted
her to go. He was determined that from now on their
lives were not going to be totally disrupted.

"We're almost there, Remy. Where do you want
me to park?

"Where should I park? Remy answer me!" he said
somewhat irritably, glancing over at her. His voice

finally penetrated through Remy's deep concentration.

Staring up and grasping for Joe's words, she asked, "What did you say?"

"I want to know where I should park," he repeated. Remy glanced around and motioned with her prayer book. "Right over there is okay. It shouldn't take too long."

The sun had risen out of Lake Michigan high above the dense diverse graph of structures outlining the sky.

A gush of warm air pressed against their backs as the Chuas entered the hospital. They took the elevator to the third floor.

Leaving the elevator, Remy and Joe passed by one of the nurses who turned and inquired, "Where have you been, Remy? You look like you haven't been feeling well."

Remy looked back and answered. "I've been off a few days, but I'm feeling better."

As they entered the respiratory department, the supervisor, Ned Ely, who was standing by his desk, noticed Remy. He pulled an envelope from his pocket.

Through her tense interior, Remy managed enough composure to say, "This is my husband, Ned."

The man smiled and gave a nod in Joe's direction. Joe smiled as he said hello. "It looks like the weather is going to be hot today," Ely said making conversation.

He paused and directed his attention to Remy. Handing her the check, his disposition changed and in a stern reprimanding tone he said to Remy, "You know the rules. If you are going to be absent, you are supposed to give notice."

"I thought it was all clear. I called and told Jennie about my condition," Remy said.

"You know better than that," he replied with disgust.

Remy's tenseness began turning into anger. She pointed her finger and blurted out, *"You haven't killed me yet!"*

Ely gave her a quizzical look.

She went on, *"You've been giving me all the difficult assignments. I'm doing more work than the others."*

"That's irrelevant," he countered. "We were discussing your absence."

Joe was watching the ensuing argument. Stepping forward and grabbing the other man's arm, he entered the altercation. "In fact, you have been working her so much that she's exhausted," he concurred and then he angrily added, "Are you willing to pay her for the time it will take her to regain her health?"

As Joe finished the statement, Ely held up his hand gesturing for him to wait. "Yes," he said looking at the thin black man behind Joe who had entered from the equipment room in the back.

Joe felt Remy's nails dig into his arm, and as he looked at her for the reason, he could see the contour of her hand in her pocket gripping her crucifix. Her anger waned and turned to fear. She looked tense and rigid.

The voice from behind Joe asked Ely, "Did the

order come in, yet? I can't get the machine cleaned without the solution."

The memory bank in Joe's brain was triggered. "That voice!" thought Joe. "I've heard it before."

As the man came closer, Ely made an attempt at formality and said, "By the way, have you met Allan Showery?"

"The name Allan," thought Joe. He stepped in front of Remy as a protective shield. His mind reeled trying to assess his approach. It came as a comment. "Oh, Mr. Showery, I understand you are an expert at karate."

He smiled. "Oh, where did you hear that?"

Although he heard the war stories were conjured and Showery had never been in VietNam, Joe continued in a contrived effort to ascertain if this was the voice on the phone.

"My wife tells me you were in Viet Nam."

"Don't remind me of Nam. It's too terrible to talk about."

Remy pulled at Joe's arm and gave him an intense anguished look. "Let's go, we've got to leave this place."

Remy rushed out of the room and Joe followed her to the elevator. On the elevator, Remy was shaking. "Breathe deeply," Joe said in a consoling tone, trying to help her regain her composure before they got off the elevator. Closing her eyes, she took the deep breaths and gave an affirmative gesture as the doors opened.

The ride home was filled with tension. They did not talk. It was not until they arrived home that they finally discussed their encounter.

Joe agonized to himself, "Was this the voice on the

phone? Is this the man? Are Remy and my family in danger? I've got to be sure."

The following morning, Guillerma had called her daughter, Lilly, to ask her to come to the Chuas'. Lilly had heard from her parents that Remy was having some kind of visions, or it had sounded like that to her, but she had not been filled in on the complete details.

The strain on the faces of the family was evident to Lilly as she sat listening to Joe tell the story. Finishing, Joe asked, "What do you think about calling the police?"

"Police!" she exclaimed. "Can you imagine calling the police? Especially being foreigners. That would be a reflection on all of us!"

"I can just see it now," Lilly mimicked, placing an imaginary phone to her ear. "Hello, I'm Dr. Chua here in Evanston, and my wife says she's been having these visions, or rather she's been possessed by the spirit of a dead woman who says she has been murdered by a man named Al. Can you imagine how that would sound?" she said exasperatedly.

"I'm a nurse. I know. Visions—possessions— that's silly! She needs a psychiatrist!"

"Psychiatrist, you say!" exclaimed Remy angrily. "My own sister thinks I'm crazy. What I'm telling you is the truth and our parents have witnessed this. How can you say that?"

She raised her arm in a sweeping direction and yelled, "Get out of my house!"

Guillerma and Vicente had watched the confrontation between the sisters and made a desperate attempt to stop Lilly. They tried to substantiate the happenings, but Lilly furiously made her way to the door. She turned back and shouted, "Joe, do as I say! Take Remy before it's too late."

"Lilly doesn't understand. She just doesn't understand what we've been through," Joe said shaking his head.

Remy calmed down. She sighed. "I don't blame Lilly for what she said. I don't believe this myself."

19

The continual days and nights of torment were grinding on Joe's nerves, and as he got up Monday morning to go to work, he sat on the edge of the bed and rubbed the back of his neck. "Thank goodness this is a short day," he thought.

"Joe," said Remy.

He looked around. "I didn't realize you were awake."

"I'm sick about what happened with Lilly. Nanang and Papang are going over to talk with her today," she said.

"I hope we can get things back to normal," Remy added wistfully.

"At least everything will have to look normal to others," Joe thought.

"Come on in, Joe, and sit down," said Terry Winograd as he opened the door to his office. He was walking with Joe Chua who had asked to speak with him about a personal matter.

Dr. Winograd allowed the taller man to sit down on the chair facing his desk, and then moved around the desk to his comfortable swivel chair. Once seated, he reached for the opened cigarette pack inside one of the pockets of his blue clinical coat. Terry tapped the packet with his fingers until a couple of cigarettes protruded. He offered Joe a cigarette, and when he declined, Terry pulled one out for himself and placed it at the side of his lips. It was then that he directed a question at Joe.

"Now, what is it that you want to talk to me about?"

"It's about my wife, Dr. Winograd."

"Her name is Re . . . Remedios, isn't it?" asked Terry, and Joe answered by nodding his head.

"Well, is she okay?" Sensing a hesitation on Joe's part to answer, he added, "You are not having any marital problems are you?"

"Oh no, it is not that." Joe almost had to smile. He went on, "Remy has been having . . . how can I say it . . . unusual psychic occurrences."

"Psychic occurrences?" Terry asked in his raspy voice. "You mean like a mental problem?"

"No, not mental—Psychic!" Measuring his words carefully, Joe went on, "Remy appears to have been possessed by the spirit of a dead woman."

"The spirit of a dead woman!" said Terry sitting up in his chair. His interest had been piqued. He snuffed out his cigarette in the ashtray, and asked, "Are you sure it is psychic? Maybe it's just a psychiatric manifestation. Perhaps, you should see someone about this."

"I have already talked to others about this," said Joe assertively.

"Was anything concluded?"

"You know how people who deal with psychiatric problems are. They go into long diatribes, more about possessiveness than possessions, but in all, I guess I got some good advice."

"What was the advice?"

"Well, maybe, not exactly advice, but it made me realize that I had to observe Remy's manifestations as a physician and not as a scared bystander."

"What exactly were your observations, Joe?" asked Terry curiously.

As Joe Chua told the story of his wife's possessions, Dr. Winograd listened intently, trying to assimilate the strange story. His fingers nervously rubbed at his mustache as he carefully scrutinized Joe. "Jose Chua had been a good addition to Franklin's staff," he thought. "He was reliable, trustworthy, and a damn good physician."

Dr. Winograd had graduated from medical school just before the Second World War began. Five years of hard work in evacuation hospitals had taught him about men under stress and human nature. He knew that what Joe Chua was telling him, as bizarre as it sounded, was true.

When Joe finished relating his story, Terry quickly said, "Joe, I wouldn't go to the police with this. Your reputation is at stake."

"I know," said Joe, "and being a foreigner in this country, they will . . ."

"I understand what you mean, Joe," interrupted Terry. "Look, why don't you try writing an anonymous letter to the police? Do something to get that dead woman off your back!"

As the day progressed for Remy, she felt more and more uncomfortable. The argument with her sister had been weighing heavily on her conscience and overshadowed her thoughts about her encounters at the hospital. She hoped that her parents would be able to explain her feelings to Lilly.

With the back of her hand, she quickly touched her forehead and cheeks. She had been repeatedly reading the passages from her prayer book. The line . . . AND MOST PAINFUL WOUND . . . was fixed in her mind as she fanned her face quickly with her hand and then swished the small prayer book back and forth in front of her face. She jerked at her red blouse sticking to her body. She went to check the thermostat. The temperature registered 70 degrees. She went to the kitchen for a glass of water. As the water ran from the faucet, she splashed it on her face.

Dabbing her face with a towel, she went to her older daughter. She said calmly, "I think you'd better get Papang and Nanang over here."

Remy then went to her bedroom.

When Guillerma and Vicente received the call from their granddaughter, they hurried back to Remy.

Joe was driving home. He mulled over what he and Dr. Winograd had discussed. "The anonymous letter might not be a bad idea," he thought.

When Vicente and Guillerma walked to the bedroom, they heard low mournful groans. "*Ohhh . . . Ohhh . . . Ohhhh . . .*"

Vicente knew the spirit was returning. He was

going to drive Teresita from his daughter. As he came into the room, Vicente grabbed from the dresser the black cloth he had carefully folded and laid two days before. Guillerma was ready to help. As Vicente handed the end of the cloth to Guillerma, Remy's head rose up.

"No, Papang, get away! Get away! Please! Just let it happen. I want to get it over with."

Vicente abided by his daughter's wish and dropped the cloth on the back of the chair and sat down. Guillerma stood by her daughter's bed silently grieving.

Vicente felt dejected. "I could've driven Teresita away," he kept thinking. From the back of his memory, a scene came forth. He was a young man back in the Philippines and he was attending an engagement party. A woman suddenly dropped to the floor. She began speaking in the voice of her dead aunt. The voice demanded that her son not marry the girl he was betrothed to, but another girl, the one he really loved. In the room, the family had hastily covered the possessed woman's body with a black mantilla and brought branches from the outside. As they hit the floor around the woman's body, the spirit seemed to be driven out of the woman, and she returned to normal.

"Why won't Remy let me help?" he agonized.

When Joe opened the door, all the girls were quietly sitting in the living room. They did not greet him, but looked towards their mother's bedroom. He heard low moans. He dropped his medical magazines and stethoscope on the couch and rushed to the bedroom. His heart began to beat faster. The moans were increasing with intensity the closer he got to the room. *"Ohhh . . . Ohhh . . . Ohh . . ."*

Vicente looked up as Joe entered the room and pushed up his black rimmed glasses, acknowledging Joe's presence.

Remy's face was red, and when Joe reached down to touch her face, he drew his hand back. Joe knew it was not a fever. Teresita was returning.

Remy opened her eyes. They looked glazed. The moans grew louder. Her arms agitated around her body. She screamed out in agony, "I'm burning!"

Joe watched in horror as she tried scraping at her flesh.

"Teresita!" Joe straightened up and planted his feet firmly on the floor. "Teresita!" he called again in a loud voice as he turned his head from side to side cautiously searching the room. "I know you are here.

"I want you to leave my wife alone! Do you understand? I want you to leave my wife and my family alone!"

There was no response, but to Joe there was a heaviness in the air about the room. She was coming closer.

Joe looked at Vicente. He was standing up. Joe sensed he had felt the atmosphere change, also.

"Damn it, I want you out of our lives!"

Joe hit his fist against his open palm venting his frustrations.

A gush of warm air radiated around Remy. He knew it was Teresita.

"Dr. Chua," the Voice sounded amplified, but calm. *"Have you done what I asked of you?"*

Joe clenched his fists. "No . . . No . . . No . . . ! Don't you understand that if I went to the police with the story you have given me, they would think that I am crazy. They won't believe me, Teresita."

"*Dr. Chua, the man Allan Showery stole my jewelry and has . . .*"

"So, he stole some jewelry, what good does that do me?"

"*Don't you understand, he gave the jewelry to his girlfriend. They live together.*" The Voice had become more stern.

"Yes, so they live together, but don't you see? How can I identify the jewelry?"

"*Estupido!*" shouted Teresita.

"*There are people who can identify my jewelry. My cousins, Ron Somera and Ken Basa, and my two friends . . . Richard Pessoti and Ray King.*

"*Call them! They will know. Ron's number is 786–4215.*"

Joe excitedly shouted to his daughter who had been standing at the door, "Hurry, get something to write that down!"

"*I bought some of the jewelry in France. And that ring, it was a gift from my father to my mother.*" The Voice began to break. "*They meant so much to me, and Al took them. Mama, Ayiii Mama!*"

Remy began agitating again.

"*Tell them that Al came to fix my television, and he killed me and burned me! Tell the police . . . Tell them.*

"*Ayiii, Ayiii, Que dolor, Mama, Mama Ayudame!*"

Tears came to Vicente's eyes. He clutched his hands together and fell to his knees. Bowing his white head, he supplicated, "Please lady . . . please . . . leave our daughter. We will help you. You have my word!"

"Yes, Teresita," said Joe firmly, "you have our word. We will help you. Now leave us in peace."

Then suddenly the room felt normal again. Teresita had left.

Joe looked down at Vicente and said, "Papang there is an Allan Showery."

Joe left the room and walked to the telephone. He was calling the police.

20

Investigator Joseph Stachula made his way through the swinging doors opening into the large room of Area 6 Homicide and went directly to his desk. As he sat down, he noticed an interoffice memo on top of his desk. It read simply: Stachula, Evanston, P.D. called this date with information on the Teresita Basa case. You are to get in touch with Dr. Jose Chua, 308 East Skokie Blvd., Skokie, Illinois, 555–2448.

Stachula rubbed his chin as he read the message over and thought, "Hm, Teresita Basa. We haven't had anything on her case since April."

The files of a murder case are never officially closed, so Stachula was elated that there might be a new piece of evidence, no matter how insignificant it might seem. Recollecting the brutal killing, he immediately decided to pursue the lead.

He knew that if the person with information was approached the wrong way, the individual could be hesitant, or even refuse, to part with the information. He did not want to lose the lead.

Reviewing the name written on the memo, he

thought that it could be a doctor who had worked with Teresita.

Settling on his course of action, he reached for the telephone and began dialing.

The line went dead.

Stachula hung up. He picked up the phone and dialed again, making sure that he was dialing the number correctly.

The line was dead.

He looked up and by the clock on the wall, he noticed it was only 5:00 p.m. It would take him, he figured, only about forty minutes to get to Skokie. He thought for a moment. With his mind made up, he headed for the garage.

Stachula slowed down his unmarked police car as he approached the corner brick ranch house. He glanced down at his memo on the car seat, double-checking the address. He saw it matched.

Parking across the street from the ranch house, the investigator got out of the car and slowly walked towards the front door, observing everything about the house.

Being a veteran of ten years with the Chicago Police Department, most of them as a plain clothes-man, Investigator Stachula was an astute observer. "It comes with the territory," he was fond of saying. The way an individual walked, dressed, talked, and his or her mannerisms, all could have a bearing on what he or she did for a living. On or off duty, he studied people and observed surroundings. It was a mental exercise he never got tired of playing.

He was at the door now, and he cleared away his thoughts as he pressed the doorbell.

In a few moments, the door inched open, just enough for the face of a serious looking Asian man, in his late thirties, Stachula calculated, to peer out at the investigator.

"Yes, can I help you?" said the man behind the door.

As the door opened wider, Stachula made a deduction as to the man's occupation: his neat appearance, from his manicured hands, he must be the doctor.

"Dr. Chua," said Stachula, and turned his usually taciturn expression into one of friendliness.

"I am Investigator Joseph Stachula of the Chicago Police Department"—flashing his police badge, and continuing—"I am here to talk with you about the Teresita Basa case."

Chua thought a moment and said, "All right— Come in, please."

With a smile still painted on his face, Stachula moved through the opened door into the house.

Once inside the house, Dr. Chua led the detective to an ornate French provincial chair at the end of the long living room.

"Please sit down, Officer," he said and then turning toward the kitchen, he called, "Remy, someone's here."

Investigator Stachula checked the room slowly, taking in all the details. The living room was tastefully decorated but sparsely furnished, and there was nothing on the walls. From his seat he could look into the dining room area and see boxes piled neatly on the floor. He assumed the Chuas had moved into the house recently. He made a mental note, strictly middle class. He focused on the door leading to a modern kitchen and could see a woman taking off an apron. She walked into the living room. She stopped when she saw the detective and glanced over to her husband with a quizzical almost frightened look.

Dr. Chua started saying, "Remy this . . ."

Before he could finish the introduction Stachula was on his feet walking towards Remy with an outstretched hand. "I'm Investigator Stachula, ma'am." He gave the woman's hand a firm shake. His observant eyes took in everything from her dark brown hair and eyes with a hint of makeup to her clothing. Stachula had a gut reaction that Mrs. Chua might have been ill recently or perhaps had gone through some personal tragedy. His mind was working overtime trying to classify the feeling he was getting about the woman.

"Please sit down, Officer," said Remy pointing back to the chair.

Stachula sat down. Deciding to stay on the offensive, he ventured, "Which one of you knew Teresita Basa?"

Remy and her husband sat down on the couch facing the investigator.

"I knew Teresita," said Remy somewhat timidly. "I didn't know her very well, but we worked on the same shifts at the hospital."

"Oh, you are a respiratory therapist, also?" asked Stachula.

"Yes sir, I have worked as a therapist ever since my husband and I came from the Philippines."

"When was that?"

"Five years ago."

"And you, Doctor," asked Stachula turning his attention to Chua. "Do you practice at Edgewater Hospital?"

"No . . . I am a physician, but I have not been licensed yet. Since I graduated from a foreign medical school, there are certain tests that I have to take. I am presently working at Franklin Park Hospital as a surgical technician."

"Franklin Park? Is that what you said?" Stachula repeated. He produced a small notebook and wrote down the notation.

He went on questioning. "Tell me Doctor, how did you come to know Teresita Basa?" Stachula watched the couple looking intently at each other. The woman dropped her stare to the floor. The way she was sitting with her hands in her lap told Stachula that she was embarrassed about something.

Dr. Chua looked at his wife, hesitated for a moment and asked, "Detective Stachula, did you talk to the Evanston Police about us?"

"What was he leading to?" thought Stachula. He answered Chua's question carefully. He did not want to lose the information now. "The Evanston Police Department told us that you possess certain information on the Basa case. However, they did not give us anything in great detail."

Dr. Chua reached into his pants pocket for a pack of cigarettes and offered the investigator one. When Stachula declined, Chua took one of the menthol tipped cigarettes for himself and lit it. He placed the matches and cigarette pack on the lamp table next to the couch and picked up a small ashtray. He held it on his knees and inhaled again on his cigarette.

"That's it," thought Stachula, "make yourself comfortable. Let's hope you're going to talk."

"Tell me," Chua began slowly, grasping for the right words, "do you believe in exorcism?"

"No . . . Joe, not exorcism," corrected Remy. "Possession!"

Stachula sensed that Dr. Chua had something important to tell him, so he replied with the standard comment, "Doctor, a good police officer has and keeps an open mind. In my work, we run into many strange things."

"As a physician, I am also trained to accept many things that can't be explained. What I am about to tell you is so bizarre that I have been hesitant to approach anyone with my story."

Chua stopped and searched the detective's face for encouragement to continue the story. He was thinking, "I hope he won't have the same reaction as the Evanston Police had and ask if Remy has ever been under psychiatric care. But they must have checked the validity of the story otherwise this detective from Chicago would not be here."

Stachula was sensitive to Chua's hesitation, and he encouraged him by saying, "Please continue Doctor, I feel that what you have to say is important to both of us."

"I understand that the police have not been actively working on the murder of Teresita."

"Well, Doctor, no murder case is ever closed until the perpetrator of the crime is caught. But, your assumptions are right. I believe that the last report on the case was on April 27th. There has been nothing new on the case for us to follow up." Stachula was leveling with him, and he hoped Chua could do the same.

Dr. Chua got up from the couch and paced a few moments. He turned to the detective and making a rotating gesture with his hand, he said, "Let's see . . . how can I tell you this?"

"Why don't you begin at the beginning, Doctor?" suggested Stachula.

Chua went back to the couch and sat down. Remy had been sitting quietly, letting her husband do all the talking.

"First of all," Chua began again, "as my wife told you, she did not know Teresita well, and I had never met the murder victim. In fact, I don't know any of the details of the murder . . . except what Teresita told me."

"You mean, your wife told you," countered the investigator.

"No sir, I mean just what I say. All I know about the case is what Teresita Basa told me."

Stachula leaned forward in his chair. "Teresita Basa told you?" he asked incredulously.

"Yes, she told me how she was killed, and who killed her."

"Who killed her? Hold it, just a moment . . . I think that you'd better tell me everything from the beginning."

21

Driving back to headquarters, Stachula reassimilated the information he had gotten from the Chuas. All of his finely tuned senses told him that the Chuas were probably telling the truth.

There was a correlation between the Chua story and what he knew. There had been no forced entry into the Basa apartment, and when he tried to catch Dr. Chua by asking him if the Voice had said anything about the rape, he had answered that she only said that she was stabbed.

"If it was the way most murders are committed," he thought, "in all probability, the victim was murdered by someone she knew."

Still, what was he going to do with the information?

He could not just walk up to this Allan Showery and arrest him. How would it sound? "I'm Investigator Stachula of the Chicago Police Department, and I'm here to arrest you on the information that we received from the woman you killed." Stachula had to laugh at that one himself.

"I can't beat this one," he said to himself. "All

these years in the force, and I thought I had seen everything."

Speeding images of the highlights in his police career raced and flickered through his thoughts.

The tumultuous summer of 1968 passed by. He was a rookie assigned to the burning west side ghettoes at the time of the Martin Luther King assassination, but after three nightmarish days and nights, he left the rubble of destruction a seasoned cop.

The scenes of the Democratic Convention and the Weathermen riots came back to him. He saw the bloodied faces of his fellow officers who had been hit by bricks and glass.

Then, an assignment to the Chicago Police Department Human Relations section had him walking a beat in the Cabrini-Green Housing Projects. During an incident at the projects, he tried to reach the bullet-riddled bodies of his friends but was caught in a barrage of crossfire and miraculously escaped death himself.

He shook his head and his thoughts snapped back to the present.

He was at headquarters, and he skillfully glided his car towards a parking space.

Turning off the engine, he made no attempt to get out of the car. He had a decision to make. He had been given some information that could be important in a murder investigation that had reached a standstill.

There would be no choice. He had to act on the information, regardless of what the source was.

Stachula got out of the car and headed into the building.

Sitting down at his desk, Stachula fed a piece of paper into the typewriter. Adjusting the carriage and aligning the paper, he began to type his report. He typed a few lines, read it, and jerked the paper out of the typewriter, crumpled it, and threw it into the wastepaper basket.

Stachula rocked back on his chair, trying to collect his thoughts. He felt that when his superiors read the report they might question his mental stability.

"The hell with it," he thought as he sat back up in his chair. He reached for a new piece of paper and quickly rolled it into the machine and began typing.

```
Page #1

Homicide/Murder
Basa, Teresita
Y-059 292
Investigation:

 The Chuas' phone was out of order so I
decided to go straight over there and try
and catch them at home.

The house sits on a corner lot, ranch style
with an attached garage. They indicated that
they had just purchased it . . .
```

When he was through typing, he had four pages of single spaced type. Stachula read them over and, satisfied with their content, walked over to the front desk near the entrance door.

Stachula handed the report to the uniformed officer and then started to return to his desk when on an impulse he went back to the desk and started writing on a piece of paper.

"One more thing," he said to the officer behind the desk. "Could you run this individual's name through to see if we have got anything on him?"

The officer quickly took the slip of paper from the investigator and said, "Sure thing, I'll put it through right away."

22

It was Thursday, the 11th of August, 1977. Three days had passed since Stachula had visited the Chuas and had written the report. Everyone in the department had read it.

Because of the serious nature of a detective's work in the homicide section, outlets to release pent-up tensions are needed. The Stachula report acted as a magnetic conduit, attracting a barrage of practical jokes and lousy ghost stories, the likes of which the department had never seen.

Stachula thought he would go crazy with all the kidding and joshing that he was getting from his fellow detectives. Tough looking men with guns holstered at their sides would mockingly tip-toe to Stachula's desk, their arms bent at the elbows and fingers rigid in an exaggerated imitation of a Hallow-een boogey man.

"Boo-hoo, Sta-hoola! Boo-hoo Stahoola!" they would say and hurry back to their desks laughing uproariously.

Their enjoyment of these shenanigans seemed to be insatiable, and Stachula had had it. "Christ sakes," he would say, "you'd think a bunch of grownup men would act their ages."

Stachula was having trouble concentrating on a report that he was working on when out of the corner of his eye he saw the tall angular form of his partner, Lee Epplen, walking towards his desk. He had a smile plastered on his face from ear to ear. "Oh no!" thought Stachula. "Please spare me one more joke."

Stachula was about to get up from his chair when Lee motioned for him to stay seated. "So help me Lee," said Stachula through his clenched teeth, "one crack out of you about the Chua report, and so help me, I'm going to . . ."

"My friend," interrupted Epplen with a condescending tone, "I bring you good tidings." He gingerly held out a paper with his thumb and forefinger.

Stachula jerked the paper from Epplen's fingers and began to read it. As he did so, a smile formed on his face and grew wider until it was as big as Epplen's. It was the information he had requested on Allan Showery. The report listed his arrest record in New York City, including two rape arrests. The two rapes had occurred in the victims' apartments, and Showery had known both of them.

Stachula noted that the address where Showery had lived at the time of the Basa murder was 445 Surf Street, less than four blocks away from the murder scene.

Stachula gave a smug look to Epplen.

"Well, what do you have to say, Joe?" inquired Epplen.

"Bingo!" said Stachula radiantly. "Bingo!"

"That's what I thought," said Epplen. "Joe, I would say that we have a good lead."

"A darn good lead!" corrected Stachula. "We have here an individual that, number one, knew the victim from work; two, has a background of rape arrests where he knows the victims; and three, he lived near the victim's apartment."

"Well, what do you think we should do?" asked Epplen.

"I think that we should go pay our Mr. Showery a visit. Let's see if he is still living at the Surf Street address."

"We don't have to do that, Joe," said Lee as he consulted his small notebook. "I already found out our friend has a new address. He lives at 630 West Schubert."

"You know, Epplen," Stachula was saying as they were walking out of the department, "sometimes I could almost get to like you."

"Please," kidded Epplen, "you are definitely not my type!"

23

The unmarked police car proceeded north passing small intersecting streets. Epplen and Stachula were discussing the unusual circumstances surrounding the case. Epplen was saying, "I got some stories from the hospital about this guy. I guess he was the one who went around the hospital collecting money for flowers for Teresita. That's nice, but I also heard that he had stolen a diamond ring off an old Jewish lady who was dying in the hospital. And another, I guess he had a way with the women . . . But, from the way you described Mrs. Chua, to use some old vernacular, she seems square."

Stachula replied, "Yeah, I think we can rule out the scorned lover theory."

The car pulled into a small street and slowed down. In the middle of the block Stachula pointed. "There it is, 630 West Schubert." They parked their car across the street in the driveway of the C.T.A. bus garage.

The detectives walked briskly across the street and up the short flight of stairs of the two story stone and frame building whose style, built at the turn of the century, was plentiful in Chicago neighborhoods. At the top of the landing was a single door, and to the right was a mail box with no name and a doorbell immediately below. Epplen pressed the doorbell a couple of times, and before long, he heard heavy footsteps moving towards the door.

Lee positioned himself to the right of the door, while Stachula moved to the left. The door opened slightly revealing a large blonde woman who was pregnant.

"Hello, ma'am, I'm Investigator Lee Epplen of the Chicago Police Department, and this is my partner, Investigator Stachula."

Looking over at the detectives for a moment and then to the badge that Epplen was holding up in his hand, the woman finally asked, "What can I do for you?"

Stachula noticed a trace of an accent in the woman's voice. "Perhaps German," he thought.

Lee went on, "We would like to talk to Allan Showery about a case we are investigating. Does Mr. Showery live here?"

The blonde woman nodded her head in the affirmative.

"Well, is he home? Can we talk with him?"

The detectives' smiles conveyed to the woman what they had intended, reassuring her they wanted Showery for nothing more serious than routine questions.

She opened the door wider and said, "Yes, Allan is here. Come on in . . . I'll get him."

The woman allowed the detectives in and quickly closed the door behind them. Motioning them towards the small living room, she pointed to a large modern couch. "Please sit down."

The two detectives sat down on each end of the couch towards the edge.

The woman left the room and returned shortly saying, "Allan will be right with you."

Both detectives were on their feet when the thin, but powerfully built, Showery came into the room. Stachula calculated Showery's age to be around thirty.

The man had a confident look about him. "Hi, what can I do for you fellows?" said Showery as he motioned for the detectives to sit down.

"Mr. Showery," started Stachula, "we are investigating the death of Teresita Basa, and we would like to talk to you about it."

"Fine," replied Showery. "What did you want to talk about?"

"Well, to tell you the truth," said Epplen, "if you wouldn't mind, we would rather talk to you at the station, rather than bothering you here at home."

"Sure," said Showery without hesitation, "I can come down to the station. When do you want to talk to me?"

"As a matter of fact," said Stachula concealing his satisfaction, "if you have some time now, we could get it over with."

Showery looked at his wife and gave her a smile and said to the detectives, "Sure, why not? Do you mind if I change these old clothes?"

"Of course, take your time," said Stachula. "We'll wait right here."

24

Showery accompanied the detectives to Area 6 Headquarters. There, he was asked to sit and wait inside one of the small interview rooms. Stachula and Epplen left the room to discuss the best way to approach the questioning of Showery.

"I think Lee, that the best way to do it is to give him the information that we got from the Chuas without giving him the source. Agree?"

"Yeah . . . let's do it," agreed Lee and opened the door to the room.

Once inside, the detectives assured Showery that it was mandatory procedure to read him his Miranda rights.

Epplen began the questioning. "Did you know Teresita Basa?"

"Oh yes, we worked on the same shift at the hospital," Showery answered, and then volunteered, "In fact, we sometimes rode the same bus home together." A confident smile crossed Showery's face.

"Allan, we have information that on the day that Miss Basa was killed you took the bus home with her. Is this true?"

"Yes, that's true."

Epplen went on. "We also have information, Allan, that on the night that she was killed, you were supposed to go and fix her television set because it wasn't working properly."

"I was supposed to fix her television set," concurred Showery, and countered, "but when we got off the bus that day, Teresita told me that she was going to do a little shopping. So I told her that I would stop home first and call back later . . . to make arrangements about coming over."

"What did she say then?" asked Epplen.

"She said that it was fine. Then I went home, changed clothes, and went out for a beer at the Roadhouse."

"The what?"

"The Roadhouse, a tavern down on Clark Street.

"I had a beer there about 5:30. I remember because the early news was coming on. So I decided to call Teresita and her line was busy and I went back and got involved in the T.V. program and talking with some people. I just forgot to call back."

Epplen looked at Stachula who had been sitting quietly with his back leaned against the wall. The two men had worked together as a team for a while and could pick up each other's signals without saying anything.

Stachula's stern expression changed to one of incredulity, and shaking his head, he spoke up, "That doesn't fit, Allan . . . it doesn't sound right. Does it, Lee?"

Lee's face had the same intense expression as Joe's. "No, not according to the information that we got."

The two detectives stared at Showery, waiting for an answer.

Stachula noticed that Showery was showing signs of being uncomfortable. His hands began gripping the seat of the chair and he started to fidget.

Epplen turned his back to Showery, ignoring him for a moment. He slowly paced the room and turned again to Showery with a fixed stare and questioned, "Have you ever been in that apartment?"

Showery procrastinated a moment and answered in a weak voice, "No, I haven't."

"We've talked to a bunch of different people that have seen you there, both socially and alone," said Epplen emphatically.

"Well, I carried her groceries into the lobby once," he responded, "maybe they saw me in the lobby."

"Allan," Epplen retorted abruptly with a note of irony in his voice, "these people know the difference between a lobby and an apartment."

"No, I was never in that apartment. I swear I was never in that apartment."

Stachula noted the beads of sweat forming on Showery's brow, and said, "Fine, Allan, you have never been in the apartment." Showery gave him a surprised look and faced Stachula. "Let's try another question." Stachula went on, "Have you ever been arrested before?"

Showery took a deep breath and said, "Yes."

"You want to tell us about it?" asked Stachula.

"There is little to tell. Some girls tried to frame me, but I was never convicted of anything."

"O.K., Allan, tell you what we are going to do," Stachula said as he got up from his chair. "We are going to take your fingerprints and compare them against those that we found in the apartment."

Showery was squirming now and sitting at the edge of the seat grasping the side of it tightly with his hands. Staring down at the floor, he said, "Go ahead . . . go ahead and do what you have to do."

"Fine," said Epplen, "we'll be back as soon as we can," and then both detectives walked out of the room closing the door behind them.

Outside the room, Epplen and Stachula discussed the progress they had made. They knew that they had caught Showery in three or four lies. The interview was going well, verifying much of the information they had obtained from the Chuas.

They had discussed the case for about five minutes when they were interrupted by a knock on the door from inside the interrogation room. The detectives looked into the room, and Showery moved back to his chair.

"What is it . . . what do you want?" asked Epplen.

"I was in that apartment," and Showery added quickly, "but I haven't been in that apartment for several months."

"Several months you say. Well, she would have cleaned in that time so your prints wouldn't be in there. Don't worry about it," said Epplen reassuringly.

Moving within Showery's radius, Stachula picked up his uncomfortableness like a radar beacon. He knew they were getting closer to the truth now and pressed on, "Are you sure it was several months ago, Allan?" emphasizing the word sure.

"No, I was there that night," confessed Showery. "But fellas, I left . . . honest. I did not have the proper tool and I did not have the schematic drawing for that particular T.V. model.

"I was in there just a couple of minutes, I left, and I never came back."

"O.K., I see. But we are going to check on it. There were a couple of beer cans found, and we are going to see if they had your prints."

Showery was visibly nervous now. "Look, I didn't go back to that apartment at all."

"Where did you go Allan? . . . I mean you had the whole evening after you left the Basa apartment. What did you do?"

Showery thought for a moment, biting his lower lip, then said, "I went back to my apartment to fix some electrical lines."

The detectives did not register an expression as Showery stood up and went on talking. "Look, if you don't believe me, go ask my wife. She'll tell you what I was doing that night. I did not go out that night!"

Epplen stepped forward and placed a friendly hand on Showery's shoulder and said, "Sit down and relax . . . think this thing through and make sure that you get your times and your places accurately."

Showery sat down obediently and looked up at Epplen. "Go talk to my wife, Yanka, she'll tell you the truth. She'll tell you," he said earnestly.

Epplen and Stachula left Showery in the interrogation room while they went back to the apartment to talk with the wife.

They rang the doorbell and waited for the door to

open. The woman looked worried when she saw the detectives. "Where is Allan?" she asked.

"Allan is back in the police station," said Epplen. "He is thinking about the night of the Teresita Basa murder, and we are hoping that you could shed a little light on his whereabouts."

"What did he tell you?" she asked letting the detectives in.

"Rather than tell you that, can you tell us anything about that night at all?"

The woman thought for a while and said, "Well I think I can because I remember the fire engine going down the streets on the way to Pine Grove."

"Do you remember what Allan was doing that night?" interjected Stachula.

"I remember that I was going to go shopping . . . yes, as a matter of fact Allan was home earlier and I had asked him if he wanted to go but he said no, so I went by myself."

Stachula's internal radar was again catching vibrations, and it told him that the girl was probably telling the truth. "And what time did you leave?" he asked.

"About seven or seven-thirty."

"Does Allan ever do any electrical work around the house?" Epplen asked.

"Electrical work? No, not that I can think of. I don't think that he knows anything about electricity."

Remembering that the Voice had told Dr. Chua that Showery had given the jewelry to his girlfriend, Stachula asked, "Are you and Allan married?"

"No, we are just living together . . . but we plan on getting married."

"Let me ask you this," said Stachula. "Has Allan ever given you any expensive jewelry presents?"

"When are we talking about?"

"Let's say from February to June. Did Allan give you any jewelry?"

"He gave me this antique ring," said Yanka and she held up her hand for Stachula's inspection.

Stachula studied the ring carefully. It appeared to be an antique cocktail ring with a pearl in the center, something like a family heirloom. It certainly didn't look like anything that Showery would buy, since judging from his clothes and furnishings, his taste ran to the modern.

"When did he give you this ring?" asked Stachula.

"I think it was the end of February or the beginning of March. He just came home one day and said, 'Baby, this is a belated Christmas present.'"

"Did he give you anything else?" asked Epplen.

"I have a jewelry box with a couple of other things he gave me."

"Look, why don't we go back to the police station and maybe we can clear up all this mess," said Epplen.

"Do I have to?" the woman asked nervously.

"No you don't have to," said Epplen reassuringly, "but Allan, he is a little scared. He said he has had some bad experiences with the police and maybe you can help straighten this whole matter out."

"Allan is really confused," added Stachula. "Right now we do not know what or who to believe."

"All right, I'll go with you. Let me get ready." As

the woman headed towards the bedroom, Investigator Stachula asked matter-of-factly, "Ma'am, is it okay if we make a call?"

The woman turned around momentarily and answered, "Yes, go right ahead."

Stachula pulled out his notebook and found the names that the Voice had said could identify the jewelry, Ron Somera and Kenneth Basa, cousins of the victim, and two of her personal friends, Richard Pessoti and Ray King.

He dialed Somera's number first, but got no answer. He then dialed Kenneth Basa's number and got a response.

"Oh, yes . . . how are you?"

"Fine, thank you. I'm calling because we have some jewelry that we want you to identify, and I was wondering if you could come to the station . . . it won't take long."

"When do you want me to come?"

"Right now, if possible."

"Well my wife isn't home yet . . . I'm babysitting, but she should be here anytime. I'll come as soon as she arrives."

Stachula's next call was to Richard Pessoti. As luck would have it, Ray King was there also and they both could come to the police station right away. Stachula replaced the phone on the receiver.

As he went to sit down, his eyes were attracted to the cover of a magazine lying on top of the corner table. He moved towards the table and picked up the magazine. It was a magazine on "Psychic Phenomenas."

He stood by the table, flipping through the magazine when Yanka, jewelry box in hand, came into the room.

Noticing the detective looking at the magazine, she asked, "Oh, are you interested in the occult?"

"No," said Stachula, as he threw the magazine on the tabletop, "but remind me to tell you an interesting story one of these days."

25

Back at the station, the detectives told Showery that they had brought his wife back with them. They noticed that seemed to calm him.

The woman was asked to wait in a large office three doors down from the corner interrogation room where Showery was waiting.

Stachula heard his name being called by the uniformed officer behind the long counter. He stepped out of the office and saw two men that he recognized as Pessoti and King. He waved for them to come to the office.

Pessoti was about to enter the room where Yanka was sitting when he froze. A shocked look entered his face. He pulled Investigator Stachula out of the small room.

"That's it! That's Teresita's cocktail ring! I'd know it any place." His voice was quivering with emotion.

Stachula then turned to King and urged, "Go take a peek and see what you think."

King moved down the short distance to the office door and glared at Yanka's hand. He came back with a positive stare and said emphatically, "That's Teresita's ring. No question about it."

Stachula went into the room and asked Yanka for the ring and her jewelry box and motioned for Epplen to follow. "We have a positive I.D., Lee," he whispered.

The detectives sat Pessoti and King by Stachula's desk and allowed them to examine the ring and the other jewelry. Both of them positively identified the ring and another piece, a jade pendant, as belonging to Teresita. There was another ring that they thought they had seen Teresita wear, but they were not absolutely certain.

Epplen and Stachula went back to Yanka holding out the jade pendant. Epplen asked, "Where did you get this piece?"

"I got that from Allan, too. It was part of the belated Christmas gift that he gave me."

"This belonged to the dead woman," said Epplen emphatically.

A look of horror registered on the woman's face. "Dead woman!" she exclaimed and began breaking into a sob. She regained her composure in a few moments and said softly, "Look, I'm telling you how I got it. I don't really know how Allan got it."

The detectives left Yanka. Outside the room, they were surprised to find Kenneth Basa busily looking over Yanka's jewelry.

"Well, what do you think?" asked Stachula addressing himself to Basa.

"No question about it, Officer. This pendant belonged to Teresita, and this ring was a gift of her father to her mother."

Basa reached into his inside jacket pocket and pulled out a pair of earrings. The match to the pendant was identical.

Stachula and Epplen walked into the interrogation room. Stachula stood in front of the seated Showery. His face was stern as he looked down at the man and said in a direct, dry tone, "Allan . . . it's all over."

Showery jumped up from the chair. "Over, what do you mean?" His eyes were darting back and forth from one detective to the other.

Epplen held out his hand revealing the cocktail ring and jade pendant resting in his palm. Showery's eyes grew large with disbelief as they focused on the jewelry.

"These belonged to Teresita Basa," said Epplen. "Why don't you tell us about what happened?"

Showery became enraged. "Everyone tries to frame me! You cops are all the same!" he shouted.

Epplen stood his ground; he remained calm, his hand still holding the jewelry.

Showery nervously stuck his hands into his pockets, and he looked away from the jewelry. "I bought those at a pawn shop," he finally said.

"What pawn shop?" Epplen asked. "Do you have a receipt? We'll check it out for you."

"No . . . no, I never got a receipt."

"Allan . . . come on," Epplen prodded. "This is a hell of a thing to keep on your chest for so long."

Showery sat down, defeated. His elbows resting on his knees, he bent down his head and began to weep.

The detectives stood back, looking down at Showery, not saying a word. Showery, his head still down, said, "Let me talk to Yanka . . . I'll tell you what happened."

"Can we be here when you talk?" asked Stachula.

"Yeah . . . I'll tell you what happened . . . but let me talk to Yanka."

Epplen went to get Yanka. He told her gently "Allan wants to talk to you."

"What happened? Is he O.K.?" asked the surprised woman as she walked towards Epplen.

"Allan wants to get something off his chest, but he wants to talk to you first," said Epplen as he escorted the woman to the interrogation room.

Yanka moved towards Showery. Stachula pulled out a chair for her and she sat in front of Showery. She held his hands and when she tried to look at him, he avoided her stare by turning his head. "Allan, what is it?"

Showery started weeping uncontrollably as if he were releasing a torrent of pent-up frustrations and guilt, and Yanka embraced him and started crying along with him.

Finally, getting his emotions under control, Showery said, " —Honey, I'm tired of fighting it. I want to get it over with." He looked up at the two silent detectives, sighed deeply, and said, "I killed Teresita Basa."

26

"On the particular night that it happened," Showery began, "I went over to Teresita's apartment at about 5:30 to look at her television set. She said that she had it fixed by some repairmen twice before . . . but they didn't know anything. When I took off the back of the set it didn't look right. So I told Teresita that I had a similar set and I would get the schematic drawings that were in my apartment and bring back some tools.

"On the way to my apartment I began to think about all the errands and things I had done for her. She would always tip me well, ten dollars or more. And there were stories around the hospital about how rich she was . . . how she was always lending money to people. I mean, it wasn't right . . . she had all that money and here I was a couple of months behind on the rent of my apartment on Surf Street. I owed money everywhere, man I was almost destitute." Showery was shaking his head. He remained silent for a long time.

"So what happened next?" encouraged Epplen.

"After half an hour or so I went to Teresita's

apartment. I mean, my mind was made up. I just knew that she had to have money and valuables in the apartment.

"I rang the doorbell and Teresita let me in. When she turned around to lock the door, I grabbed her from behind in a Japanese half-nelson."

"A Japanese half-nelson?" asked Epplen.

"Yeah, like this." Showery got up and brought up his muscular arm demonstrating the choke hold. "I know about martial arts," he went on as he sat down, "and Teresita was out in a minute."

"What did you do then?" asked Stachula.

"I laid her down in the front room and I found her purse. It only had thirty dollars! I then dragged her into the bedroom."

"Was she still unconscious?" asked Epplen.

"Yeah . . . she was out like a light. Anyway, I took off all her clothes."

"Allan, did you rape her?" asked Epplen.

"No . . . no, I just wanted to make it look like rape, that's why I spread her legs apart."

Listening to Showery's statement, Stachula realized that only a handful of people knew that Teresita had not been raped. The killer was one of them. When his mind began to focus on the confession again he could hear Showery saying and motioning to his chest, "I stabbed her right here in the sternum with the kitchen knife."

Stachula caught Epplen's eyes; he seemed to be telling him, "Can you believe this? The Voice that spoke to the Chuas was right."

Showery went on, "After I made sure that the mattress had caught on fire, I turned it over on the body. Then I left . . . nobody saw me leave."

Showery was exhausted, his emotions spent. The stillness in the room was interrupted by the voice of Investigator Epplen, who also sounded tired and emotionally drained. "Allan, I am going to bring in the state's attorney . . . he will want to take a full confession. Are you ready for that?"

"Yes . . . yes I am," said Showery with some finality in his voice.

Epplen left to make a phone call and in a matter of minutes an assistant state's attorney, along with a court reporter, came from their office which was also located in Area 6 headquarters.

After being briefed by the detectives, the state's attorney went into the interrogation room.

The tall, serious looking lawyer walked towards Showery. Adjusting his metal-rimmed glasses, he said, "Mr. Showery, I am Assistant State's Attorney Paul Linton and this"—he was pointing to a young woman who was busily setting up her transcribing machine—"is Miss Blanca Lara, a court reporter. I understand that you want to make a statement. Is that correct?"

Showery nodded his head.

"Mr. Showery," said Linton, "you will have to speak up so that our reporter can hear you."

"Yes . . . I want to tell you what happened."

"Good . . . but before we begin, I have to inform you that," Linton's voice changed to a monotone as he recited, "you have the right to remain silent and to refuse to answer any questions. Anything that you say can and will be used against you in a court of law . . ."

Epilogue

Shortly after the news of Allan Showery's arrest, Señora Basa died in Dumaguete.

In lieu of a $500,000 bond, Showery was held seventeen months in Cook County Jail until the trial.

Remy no longer feared for her life.

The press had picked up the story, and it had become front page news.

The Chuas were greatly troubled by the publicity associated with their involvement in what had become known all over the country and world as the Voice From the Grave case. They were concerned that their children and family would be ridiculed.

In March of 1978, the Chuas prepared for their daughter's cotillion. It was an important event for their family and a welcome relief. Their lives were getting back to normal.

An article with a picture of their daughter appeared in a newspaper stating that Ms. Chua was being presented at the cotillion and the unusual aspect to the story was that she was the daughter of Remedios Chua who was the possessed lady in the notorious Voice From the Grave case. Remy wept with her daughter as she read the article. It was heartbreaking for Remy to see that her daughter was being involved. The daughter pondered about the adverse publicity, and made a decision that she would attend the cotillion.

They took many pictures of the memorable occasion with the daughter in a white tulle and lace princess gown, contrasting with her long black hair, Joe in a tuxedo, and Remy in a delicate lace gown.

No matter how insignificant it might have seemed to others, to them, they had passed a barrier and would be able to cope with whatever lay ahead.

Remy and Joe Chua became citizens of the United States in November of 1978.

At the Naturalization Hearing, a black judge presided in the crowded courtroom. He drew applause when he told the story of being a son of an immigrant himself, and how proud he was to be presiding over the hearing for the new citizens.

Everyone in the room was moved by the inspiring speech. To Remy, it imparted inspiration that the United States was truly a land of opportunity for all and there was hope for future generations.

On January 21, 1979, during one of the worst winters in Chicago history, the trial of Allan Showery began.

The prosecutors for the State of Illinois were Thomas Organ and Lee Schoen. Three public defenders were assigned to represent Showery. They were William Swano, Daniel Radakovich, and Karen Thompson.

The jury was composed of eight men and four women who heard the evidence presented in the courtroom of Judge Frank W. Barbaro.

Barbaro, a distinguished judge with thirty-two years of experience as a lawyer, sixteen of those serving on the bench, had heard almost every conceivable story in his courtroom. The story of Teresita Basa, however, was his most unusual case.

The prosecution had rested its case. They had tried to avoid calling the Chuas for testimony, but in a surprise move, Defense Attorney Radakovich called on the Chuas.

Remy Chua testified before an intensely quiet courtroom during the fourth day of the trial. Remy realized she feared nothing as she looked directly at Showery and he at her.

Joe Chua gave short direct answers to the questioning.

The family avoided the nightly newscasts that religiously reported the proceedings since the trial had attracted worldwide attention. The trial lasted for eight days. The attorneys for each side had adeptly presented their cases. The jury heard a total of thirty-three witnesses. Late on Wednesday of the 24th, the jury began their deliberation.

On Friday, the 26th of January, after thirteen hours of deliberation, the jury reported that it was hopelessly deadlocked.

When the Chuas heard the news of the mistrial, they were concerned that Showery might seek revenge if he were set free. Remy Chua had repeatedly

told the prosecuting attorney, Thomas Organ, that
she had no personal malice against Showery.

She was only relating Teresita's story.

Almost four weeks had passed since the mistrial,
and Remy and Joe were discussing what could be
happening.

"Joe, I am worried about the new trial. I hate to
testify again. They will try again to make it seem
like the story of Teresita is not true."

Joe reflected and answered, "Teresita must have
had a reason for picking us to tell her story. She
works in strange ways, and I don't think that she
will let us down."

On Friday, February 23, 1979, two years after the
murder, in the courtroom of Judge Barbaro, Allan
Showery pleaded guilty. Showery had entered the
plea of guilty against the advice of his lawyers who
wanted him to stand a second trial.

A sentence was imposed of fourteen years for
murder and four years each, for two counts of armed
robbery and arson.

The Chuas had been vindicated.

Teresita Basa could rest in peace.